"Volper's chapters or _____ gic networking, sales presentati _____ he best I have ever read. His other chapters are also jam-packed with dozens of actionable ideas for both senior executives and their sales teams. Our company has had the pleasure of working with Ron, and I can only say that he is a genuine thought-leader. Many of his most innovative ideas are found between the covers of this gem of a book."

—Stanley Freimuth, chief operating officer (ret), Fujifilm USA; chairman, Tracer Imaging

"Up Your Sales in a Down Market is the most timely and useful sales book on the market today. Ron Volper has helped us dramatically increase our company's sales, and this book captures many of his best ideas from his 30 years as a sales executive, VP of Sales, and sales consultant."

—Lonnie Ferrell, SVP Customer Care and Operations, WhiteFence Inc.·

"Up Your Sales in a Down Market is jam-packed with great ideas to win over cautious customers in tough times and good times. As EVP of Sales and Marketing, my company and I have measurably benefited from our long-standing partnership with Ron and the Ron Volper Group. Even veteran CEOs and sales and marketing executives will be blown away by Volper's new ideas to increase sales."

—John A. Thornton , executive vice president of Sales and Marketing, Amalgamated Life Insurance Co.

"Ron Volper's sales techniques and skills are unmatched and have helped us achieve extremely aggressive revenue goals during the past 15 years. In 2010, Jefferson National was named the Financial Services Company of the Year due to our extraordinary growth during the Great Recession, and Ron's contributions were a large part of our success. *Up Your Sales in a Down Market* is a must read because it contains Ron's unique ideas and proven sales strategies."

—David Lau, chief operating officer,
Jefferson National Insurance

"Ron Volper's sales and marketing recommendations played a major role in increasing our sales and contributed to our company's successful IPO. With priceless advice and powerful examples, *Up Your Sales in a Down Market* is a must for executives and salespeople needing to win over cautious customers in a tough economy."

—Lawrence Miller, president and CEO,
StoneMor Partners L.P.

"*Up Your Sales in a Down Market* is the only book I know of that tells both salespeople and executives who manage them what they need to do differently to win over cautious customers in tough times. Volper's ideas are based on his firm's research and on his own successful experience in running sales and marketing. Our bank has benefited from working with him in the training of sales staff during a new product launch. These ideas are clearly laid out in his outstanding book."

—Richard O. Jones, executive vice president, Business
Services, Provident Bank

"Volper's book is jam-packed with great information and ideas to help any salesperson beat the competition and increase his sales. His strategy on questioning is the best I've ever seen. And he pinpoints exactly what senior executives now need to do to support their sales teams and help them win over cautious customers, and protect those relationships. My sales team loved the custom sales training he conducted for our company, and we've all benefited from working with him."
—Matthew M. Grove, vice president, Guaranteed Lifetime Income, New York Life

"Ron's new book is fantastic: it's clear, concise, and cogent. For the first time someone has recognized the need to segment the customer base into different subsets of personalities. Ron's book provides amazing insights into the nuances needed to win over different customer types in a tough economy. A must read for sales execs!"
—Richard Gaccione, president and CEO, Pay-O-Matic

"Volper's sales and service audit, and his training for our company, were invaluable. Volper's book distinguishes itself, because he offers both salespeople and executives practical strategies to plan and make sales. His innovative approach is grounded on his firm's proprietary research. This book is a highly usable tool as it is clearly written and jam-packed with original ideas."
—Carla Romita, senior vice president, Castle Oil Company

"The chapter on building a customer-centric organization in *Up Your Sales in a Down Market* is the best I have ever read on getting customers and turning them into advocates for your company. And the 19 other strategies that Volper recommends are similarly powerful. Among the many things that distinguish this book is that Volper's recommendations are based not only on his own experiences as a salesperson and head of sales, but on his firm's extensive research on how to sell when customers are afraid to buy."

—Jonathan Merrill, vice president, Acquisitions and Development, Time Equities, Inc.

"I've read dozens of marketing and sales books, but none is as thoughtful and thorough as *Up Your Sales in a Down Market*. The chapter on planning sales and segmenting the customer base offers the best advice I've ever seen on selling more to fearful customers in tough times and good times. In today's market, it should be a must read for every CEO, entrepreneur, and sales and marketing executive."

—Drew Neidorf, former president, CIT Credit Finance

"Ron Volper's impressive Fortune 500 sales career forms the basis for his even more successful role as one of the nation's leaders in sales consulting and sales training. *Up Your Sales in a Down Market* tells senior executives and salespeople how the author has developed and expanded customer relationships, and what they need to do to penetrate their key markets in these uncertain times."

—Paul J. Massey Jr., CEO and founding partner, Massey Knakal Realty Services

"In today's turbulent business environment, where so many customers are afraid to 'pull the trigger,' Volper's book offers both executives and business developers proven strategies and ideas to accelerate sales revenues and create more value for their customers. It's clearly and concisely written and is destined to become a business classic. *Up Your Sales in a Down Market* is a must read."

—John M. Tolomer, president and chief executive officer, The Westchester Bank

Up Your
Sales
in a
Down Market

20 Strategies From Top
Performing
Salespeople to Win Over
Cautious Customers

By Ron Volper, PhD

THE CAREER PRESS, INC.
Pompton Plains, NJ

UP YOUR SALES IN A DOWN MARKET
EDITED BY JODI BRANDON
TYPSET BY EILEEN MUNSON
Cover design by Matt Simmons
Printed in the U.S.A.

To order this title, please call toll-free 1-800-CAREER-1 (NJ and Canada: 201-848-0310) to order using VISA or MasterCard, or for further information on books from Career Press.

The Career Press, Inc.
220 West Parkway, Unit 12
Pompton Plains, NJ 07444
www.careerpress.com

Library of Congress Cataloging-in-Publication Data
CIP Data Available Upon Request

To my wife
Hillary
whose loving support
made this book—and so much else—possible.

This book could not have been written without the help of many others. My talented agent, Jeff Herman, of Jeff Herman Associates, deserves my thanks for finding the book a great home with Career Press, and for his wise counsel.

I am grateful to my good friend and colleague Don Gabor, who has provided me with encouragement and countless suggestions that improved the organization of the book.

I would like to thank Adam Schwartz, the acquisitions editor, and his colleagues at Career Press for their confidence in me and for their helpful advice. I would especially like to thank Kirsten Dalley and Jodi Brandon, my able editors at Career Press, and their colleagues, for reading the manuscript and offering valuable suggestions.

Finally, I would like to thank the clients of Ron Volper Group—*Building Better Sales Teams*—for their encouragement and for letting us work with their executives and sales teams before and during the writing of this book.

Contents

◇

Preface

The recommendations in *Up Your Sales in a Down Market* are based on my experiences of more than 30 years as a salesperson, sales manager, vice president of sales and marketing for a Fortune 500 company, advisor on business development, and sales trainer for more than 90 Fortune 500 companies and nearly three hundred other businesses—in good and tough times. My recommendations for changing sales tactics and strategies are supported not only by anecdotal information, but by my firm's proprietary "Sales Analytics" in which we collected, analyzed, and compared information based on:

» Sales reports for our clients' sales team and individual salespeople.

» What salespeople tell us they say and do before, during, and after meeting with customers.

» What managers tell us their salespeople do.

» What customers report salespeople say and do.

» What we observe salespeople saying and doing on sales calls.

We compared top-performing salespeople—those who exceeded their revenue and other sales goals—with their peers who had not met their revenue and sales goals. In addition, we compared the activities and results of the two groups in both rising and falling markets. Examples of the questions we investigated included:

» How many calls and to which decision-makers do salespeople make calls?

» What is the revenue per call?

» What is the mix of new business versus repeat business?

» How many contacts does it take to gain an appointment and to close a sale?

» How many accounts does a salesperson handle?

» What type of questions does a salesperson ask?

» What goals does a salesperson set for a call, and how does the salesperson ask for the customer's commitment?

Similarly, as part of our ongoing work with our clients, we gathered data about what sales managers and executives at sales-driven companies do differently from other companies when markets are up and down. Examples of the questions we investigated for sales managers and their companies included:

» How do they recruit and select salespeople?

» How do they measure and manage salespeople?

» How do they train and coach salespeople?

» What tools do they give salespeople?

» How do they compensate salespeople?

» How do they motivate salespeople?

A Definition Before We Begin

I use the term *market* in this book in a particular context. When I refer to *market,* I do not mean the overall economy or financial markets. Instead, I mean the specific group of accounts, geographical area, or industry—the territory—that a salesperson has been assigned. If a salesperson has not yet reached his numbers, we can say that his market is down.

You Can Sell More Even When Your Market Is Down

Up Your Sales in a Down Market is based on proven sales practices that have worked for me and my clients. And nothing will make me happier than having these strategies work for you, too, no matter how the economy is affecting your customers. So if you're ready to increase your sales—even when your market is down—let's get started.

Introduction

Customers change their buying behavior when good times become bad times, and salespeople need to change their sales approach if they are to succeed in both environments. *Up Your Sales in a Down Market* explains why and how customer behavior changes in a tough economy, and tells salespeople, sales managers, and senior executives how to change their sales strategies and tactics before, during, and after meeting with customers.

When their businesses are struggling, many customers may be gripped by fear and often buy less and later. And because salespeople whose markets are down and are behind in their numbers may be worried that they will not get the sale, they run the risk that they will inadvertently pressure customers and exacerbate their fears. There is little doubt that today's customers are more skittish and that their buying behavior has dramatically changed. Some of the dynamics that shift the balance of power to customers and make a seller's job harder when their individual markets are down are:

> » Customers are more afraid of making the wrong decision when budgets are tight.
> » Buying decisions that were previously made by individuals are made by buying committees or at a more senior level.

» Customers are more likely to put greater emphasis on price and solicit quotes from multiple vendors, including ones located thousands of miles away.

» In a strong economy, customers might only ask about the return on their investment, whereas in a weaker economy, more customers demand proof of sellers' claims.

» Customers are less willing to implement a recommended program in its entirety without first testing the product or service and evaluating its benefits before committing to it.

» Customers are less likely to rely on what sellers tell them and are more motivated to research information from third parties and the Internet, and they may know as much about a given product as the seller of that product.

This Book Will Help Salespeople and Sales Managers Succeed in a Down Market

Up Your Sales in a Down Market shows salespeople and sales managers how to use different strategies and tactics to find customers, develop and deepen customer relationships, and increase sales in a tough economy. It pinpoints how to meet the challenges of selling to customers who are grappling with an ever-changing economy. And because even top-performing salespeople do not succeed without a sales organization to support them, *Up Your Sales in a Down Market* also spells out what sales managers and senior executives can do to build a customer-centric sales culture that will guarantee them loyalty and profits from their customers.

In **Part I: Strategies to Help You Sell More to Cautious Customers,** *salespeople* will learn practical skills and easy-to-implement strategies that will enable them to:

» Convince reluctant customers to make buying decisions.

» Build rapport with wary customers.

» Ask questions to uncover apprehensive customer needs and concerns.

» Offer low-risk recommendations to hesitant customers.

» Overcome objections of risk-averse customers.

» Gain commitment from unenthusiastic customers.

» Give sales presentations that convince hard-to-win-over customers.

» Deliver proposals to exacting customers.

» Enlist customers to help you develop new business.

» Practice sales habits that appeal to cautious customers.

Additional sales strategies and tips can be found on my Website (*www.ronvolpergroup.com*).

In **Part II: Strategies to Help Your Sales Team Sell More to Cautious Customers,** *sales managers* will learn practical and easy-to-implement strategies that will enable them to:

» Create and develop a customer-centric sales team.

» Deliver training programs that increase their sales team's revenue.

» Coach their sales team to achieve its sales goals.

» Make every sales meeting motivating and productive.

» Recruit and hire top producers for their sales team.

» Realign and reassign territories to boost their sales team's revenue.

» Protect their sales reps' "Golden Selling Hours."

» Maximize their sales team's intellectual capital, so they can adapt their sales approach.

» Increase their sales team's performance with motivating and flexible compensation plans.

» Recognize, reward, and inspire their entire sales team.

So whether you are a newcomer to the sales profession, a seasoned pro, a sales manager, or a VP of sales, you will more readily achieve your goals when you follow the advice and the tested practices of the top performing salespeople in *Up Your Sales in a Down Market.*

P<u>art</u> I

Strategies to Help

You Sell More to

Cautious Customers

Strategy 1

Zero in on Your Cautious Customers

*There is a twenty-five times greater likelihood
that an existing customer will buy more from
you than a prospect will buy anything from you.*
—Ron Volper Group 2010 Sales Study

The year 1977 was special for me. It was my first year as a sales executive at a Fortune 500 company, but I outsold my colleagues and was named "Salesperson of the Year." In recognition of that achievement, I was awarded the use of a new Mercedes-Benz for the following year. That was a proud moment. As we entered the final quarter of my second year, I kept thinking of the old adage "lightening doesn't strike twice in the same place" and that there was no way that I would be able to outsell the savvy veterans at my company again. But I did! My boss, who was not big on recognition, said, "Ron, you get to keep the car for another year." Being a brash young kid at the time, I asked if I could have a new car, and in short order my black Mercedes was replaced by a shiny new silver one.

As I entered the fourth quarter of year three, I was sure that I would always be driving a company-paid Mercedes, but I was in for a rude surprise. Another salesperson outsold me—by a lot—and my beloved Mercedes was taken from me. Although my car was never involved in an accident, I crashed when I learned that I had been deposed as Salesperson of the Year. Soon afterward, I did some soul searching and thought about why I sold more in my first and second years (when I knew less) than in my third year (when I knew more). Here's what I discovered.

Use a M-O-R-E Strategy

In year three, I became overconfident and gave short shrift to one of the most essential elements of sales success: sales planning. Looking back, I realized that I sold more in my first two years because I used what I now call the *M-O-R-E strategy*. I divided my accounts into four buckets, each represented by the letters in the word *more* (M-O-R-E).

M = Maintain Current Customers

The letter *M* in M-O-R-E means *maintain current customers*. It represented those accounts my company was already doing business with and whose relationships I needed to protect when my markets were up and when they were down. I thought about the time I splurged for a thousand-dollar raffle ticket and did not win. I was disappointed but not crushed. Then I thought about the time someone stole my coin collection, which was valued at about $1,000. In that instance, I was in a rage. And that thought caused me to realize that it's often more painful to lose something we have (including an existing account relationship) than to not get something we do not yet have.

Another reason for maintaining current relationships, especially if you are behind in your sales, is that there is a 25-times-greater likelihood that an existing customer will buy more from you than a prospect will buy anything from you (according to the Ron Volper Group 2010 Sales Study). So for each of my existing 20 accounts, I conducted what I now call a *Vulnerability Analysis*. I created a grid and listed:

> » How long we had been doing business with that customer.

» The last time they had used our services.

» Whether their order size was trending upward or downward.

» How many of our products/services they used.

» How the decision-makers, influencers, and users perceived us, and why.

» How many referrals they had given us.

» The last time we had been in touch with them.

I also thought more generally about what might be some early warning signals that a given customer's enthusiasm for my company might be waning, so I developed a list of early warning signals. Some of these signals are industry-specific and even account-specific, but others are generic. Here are some examples:

» They return phone calls less quickly than previously or not at all.

» You have more trouble getting in to see them, or the meetings are less cordial and more perfunctory.

» They ask you questions or voice objections to your product or company that you have already responded to.

» They order or use less of your product.

» They do not honor commitments they have made to you.

» They involve new people in the decision process.

» They treat you like a stranger when you thought you were family.

For example, I helped one of my clients, a major regional bank, apply this Vulnerability Analysis. I worked with them to identify any of their business customers where the monthly activity in their checking accounts was lower than usual, thus signaling a potential problem.

Conduct Account Reviews

The second action I took to maintain customers in years one and two of my sales career that I was less diligent about in year three was to conduct formal account reviews. Of my 20 existing accounts, all but one agreed to meet with me; and in 15 of the 19 accounts I met with, the decision-makers and decision-influencers attended the review. This represented a great way for me to meet the key players. In these account reviews, I did the following:

- » Told them about my background and how I could personally provide added value to them.
- » Thanked them again for the business.
- » Verified how they would measure the value they derived from our company's consulting services.
- » Identified how well we were meeting and exceeding their expectations.
- » Gave them some additional ideas as to how to more effectively use our products.
- » Surfaced needs for additional products.
- » Gave them my home phone number (at a time when cell phones and e-mail did not exist) and encouraged them to call me at any time.

The definition of the word *customer* comes into play here. At a time when there is so much turmoil in corporate America and elsewhere, and when so many employees change jobs, there is a good chance that your contact at a given company is no longer there. If you as a salesperson have not been in touch with the account for more than six months, they may no longer think of themselves as a customer. That is why, as part of your *maintain* strategy, you should be in touch with every customer at least twice annually; for better customers, quarterly; and for "A" accounts (customers that give you a large chunk of your business or have the potential to do so), at least monthly and sometimes even more often.

Use an Impact Management Strategy

How often you contact customers and potential customers and how you create top-of-mind awareness (face-to-face meetings, entertainment, telephone calls, e-mails, letters, cards, and so forth) constitute your *Impact Management Strategy.* Salespeople who are in the top 10 percent of producers not only contact their accounts more often, and do so through many different channels, but also plan on a quarterly basis which accounts they should call on, and for what purpose.

O = Obtain New Business

The second part of my M-O-R-E strategy was—and still is—represented by the letter *O*: *obtain new business.* As most salespeople do, I often had difficulty reaching prospects on the phone. My analysis revealed that I was only able to get through to approximately 5 percent of people who did not know me. What I did not know at the time was that salespeople typically reach only 2 percent of prospects who don't know them, so I was actually doing well.

What was even more compelling, however, is the following: I asked the people who gave me referrals to contact the person to whom they referred me and tell that person that I would be calling, and when they did so, my call completion rate jumped to 60 percent. Here, too, my earlier experience has been confirmed more recently by our firm's 2010 Sales Study. A referral is four times more likely to result in the prospect taking your call than if you call cold. And if you get an introduction, you are three times more likely than with a referral to have cautious customers take your call. So if you're not getting the new business you want, remember the numbers: 2 percent, 20 percent, and 60 percent. Ask virtually everyone you can for a referral and, if possible, for an introduction.

Many salespeople, and especially ones behind in their numbers, agonize over when the best time to ask a contact for a referral is. The answer is now. Other than on those rare occasions when a customer is unhappy with something you've done or failed to do, there is no time like the present. Having said that, an especially propitious time to ask is when you know the customer is pleased with the results of your product or service, or when the customer says something positive about you or your company. And don't be shy about asking for an introduction once you get the referral.

One approach that has helped me convert referrals into introductions is to offer to host a breakfast or lunch for the three of us. One discovery I made is that many customers are willing to give salespeople a referral after they have declined their offer to do business. If you have established rapport with them, they may want to be helpful and may open up their "Rolodexes" to you. If you ask in a warm and respectful way, without seeming desperate, you can obtain some referrals and introductions from customers and others, even if they have not bought from you. And if you go out of your way to help them, they will be even more willing to reciprocate with referrals, introductions, and information.

R = Recover Former Relationships

A third strategy I used to drive incremental revenue is represented by the letter *R* in M-O-R-E: *recover former relationships.* Unlike most of my peers, I went back and contacted former customers, starting with the largest and most recent ones. After all, these were customers who were familiar with my company, and even knew how to order and use our products. I reasoned that if I could win back even one of them, I might not have to spend as much time hand-holding them. As it turned out, I was able to obtain a six-figure contract from one and a high-five-figure contract from another, all because I was willing to reach out to them.

My recommendation for all salespeople, especially for salespeople in need of a quick win, is to scour your database for former customers and call them. If they are no longer

customers because they
company did or failed to

» Identify exactly wh

» Apologize for it.

» Explain what you a
will do so the prob

It is also helpful to h
pany call a C-level execut
apologize for the problem

tomers are no longer doing business with your company not
because of any dissatisfaction with your company, but because
a competitor offered a lower price or offered a product that at
the time more closely met their needs. In many instances, you
can win back customers and build your sales in less time than
it takes to develop a new customer relationship.

E = Expand Existing Relationships

The fourth and last channel to grow revenues, especially
when your business is sluggish, is to *expand existing relationships*
with current customers. This is represented by the letter *E* in
M-O-R-E. In my third year in sales, one of the reasons I lost
my Mercedes was that I was not scrupulous about approaching
all my existing customers to identify additional opportunities.
If you're not hitting your sales goals, it may indicate that you're
not exploiting the three ways to expand relationships. These
are:

1. Sell more of your current products to a given "buy
   center" (department, and so forth).

2. Cross-sell additional products to an existing buy
   center.

3. Sell your products to a different buy center in the
   same company (this could mean a different
   department, division, affiliate, subsidiary, and so on).

s usually easier to obtain an introduction
al to your customer's colleague in the same
to someone in another company who might
customer's competitor.

e Ways to Jump-Start Sales
se Account Plans

Another way to use M-O-R-E strategies to jump-start sales is to build and use an *account plan* for each of your key accounts. In your account plan list your quarterly objectives and longer-term objectives, the decision-makers and influencers, the products and resources that will help satisfy their needs, and your competition. Even though you will likely change your account objectives and strategies over time, it is important that you make your plan as specific and as measurable as possible by including sales tactics, dates, and dollar projections.

2. Conduct a Wallet Share Analysis

Though I never returned to the number-one spot as the top-performing salesperson at my company, in my fourth year and subsequently, I was in the top 1 percent of performers among a large and talented group of sales executives. One of the ways I got back on track and restored my reputation was to develop and use a tool I call a *Wallet Share Analysis* for my "A" accounts or those accounts that had the potential to become "A" accounts. Whereas many of my colleagues were happy that certain accounts they called on gave them a substantial percent of their business, I was not. I wanted to know what percent of their total business my firm was getting. Although a few customers were reluctant to tell me, 90 percent of them willingly shared this information. Armed with this data, I was in a position to know not only what percent of my business a given account represented but, more importantly, what percent of their business my firm had captured, and what our additional potential was.

As a result, in instances where we may have been doing a large amount of business but were still leaving money on the table for our competitors, I was often able to identify why. This not only served as valuable information for our new product development and marketing executives, but helped me learn more about their needs and develop incremental business from a number of customers.

3. Use a Pipeline Report

A final recommendation to get your sales back on track and moving at the right speed is to complete and use a monthly *Pipeline Report,* also known as a "Front-log and Forecast." Although many sales executives and their companies use such a tool, only the top 10 percent of salespeople maximize its value. The Pipeline Report gives you a bird's-eye view of your territory and serves as a guide to help you allocate the appropriate amount of time and resources to the most productive opportunities. Simply put, it prevents you from squandering time on accounts with a low probability of closing or that have low revenue potential. And it insures that you will not overlook those accounts that have a high likelihood of closing and/or represent large upside revenue potential.

Use M-O-R-E Strategies to Stay Focused on Your Sales Goals

With so many competing demands on your time, and if you happen to be behind in your revenue, it is understandable that you would want to drive yourself harder, but before you go faster, make sure you are going in the right direction. Whether you drive a Mercedes or a Ford, the M-O-R-E strategies and sales planning tools described in this strategy can serve as your GPS, and help you raise your sales in a down market.

Strategy 2

Build Rapport Before Selling to Wary Customers

Top-performing salespeople recognize when customers have curtailed budgets; they need more reassurance to overcome their fear of making wrong buying decisions.
—Ron Volper Group 2010 Sales Study

Some years ago, a young salesperson was calling on the executive vice president of marketing at a global pharmaceutical company. As part of his rapport-building, the salesperson asked the EVP a number of questions about his interests outside of business. Apparently because he made this executive feel comfortable, the EVP shared some personal information about himself, and, in turn, asked the salesperson questions about himself. When the salesperson mentioned the name of the town where he lived, the EVP revealed that he was getting married and that his wife-to-be always wanted to live in that suburb in New York, but there were almost no homes on the market when he looked.

The sales call ended inconclusively, and, as he was driving home, the salesperson was scratching his head trying to figure out a next step with this prospect. As he neared his home, he spotted a "For Sale" sign in front of a home a few blocks from his own—and the lights went on (not in that home, but in his head). Early the next morning, the salesperson called the EVP, who was so pleased to get this "lead" that he invited the salesperson to join him for lunch later in the week. And a week later, the EVP and his bride signed a contract to buy the house.

Although there were many factors at play, the salesperson ultimately succeeded in closing a half-million-dollar contract for sales consulting services with the EVP because he had built rapport with the EVP and demonstrated that he would go out of his way to be helpful to him. As the producer of that contract, I never thought of myself as a real estate scout, but by building rapport with that executive and going out of my way to help him, I was able to make both a new friend and a new customer. In fact, his company became my largest account that year. This experience taught me that *saying* the right thing is helpful, but *doing* the right thing is essential for building rapport.

The Elements of Rapport

Rapport with customers has two elements. First, the customer finds the salesperson likeable and comfortable to be with. Second, the customer trusts the salesperson. In the wake of many high-profile business scandals, many customers are now less trusting of salespeople who over-promise and under-deliver. But our survey of customer perceptions of salespeople confirms that there is a direct correlation between top-producing salespeople and customers' positive perceptions of them. To build rapport and counteract customers' fears about making the wrong decision, top salespeople are more:

» Helpful.

» Available.

» Patient.

» Reassuring.

» Empathetic.

Be Helpful

Here is an example of how a struggling salesperson at a global IT consulting company went out of his way to help a customer and thereby turned around his numbers. The salesperson learned that his customer, the company's CFO, was laid off from her job, and even though ironically this salesperson was worried about losing his own job because his sales were down, he took the time to introduce the CFO to his friend at a search firm and called every few weeks to offer encouragement. When the former CFO saw how helpful the salesperson was, she began to confide in him and mentioned that she had an upcoming interview for a position as the CFO at a major chemical company.

The salesperson realized that, coincidentally, he knew a senior executive at that company, and he put in a good word for the candidate. Ultimately, his former customer was offered and accepted a position there. And though there was no obligation for his former customer to do so and even though the company was tightly managing its expenses, soon after they hired the CFO candidate, the company signed a seven-figure contract for the IT services of the salesperson's firm, and the "struggling salesperson" emerged as a hero at his company.

Be Available

Some years ago, a major telecommunications company our firm was in discussions with was ranked near the bottom in independent customer service surveys. So I proposed that my firm develop a training program on customer service skills for their customer contact people and managers. When the executive vice president of consumer markets called with a question about our proposal, my assistant told her I was on a hiking trip in a remote part of Alaska and that she might not be able to reach me for several days. By chance, I happened to call my office a few minutes later, and I immediately returned my prospect's call. She said she was so impressed with my availability—even while I was on vacation—that she committed to the project on my phone call from Denali Park, Alaska.

In the early 1980s in a down market, PNC, a major Pennsylvania regional bank, grew dramatically and gained market share. At a time when cell phones were not widely used, the executive vice president of retail banking there had his home telephone number printed on his business cards, and encouraged customers to call him at home. Though this was not the major factor contributing to the bank's growth, it did signal to customers that he and his team would go out of their way to be there for them—and they were.

Be Patient

Salespeople who have not yet reached their goals also need to recognize that, although customers expect an immediate response to their requests, these same customers may be inundated with work and may not respond as quickly to *their* recommendations. So they should not assume that a delay means that the customer is not interested in talking with them.

I recently spoke to the owner of a large real estate company that I had had a productive breakfast meeting with three months previously. At our breakfast meeting, he said he would set up a meeting with his brother, the co-owner, for the following week. I called him 10 times and sent several e-mails without getting through. On the 11th attempt, two months later, I finally reached him. After apologizing for not getting back to me, he explained, "I was so embarrassed about not having the time to return your calls, Ron, that when I finally did have time I was too uncomfortable to do so."

Top salespeople are more patient and, as a way to create trust, often do the following:

>> Suggest that the customer first use the product on a trial basis.

>> Arrange for the customer to speak to a satisfied user.

>> Agree to another meeting with the contact's boss.

>> Present additional information showing the return on investment.

>> Provide documentation for any claims.

>> Create less costly or risky alternatives.

Acknowledge Customers' Time Constraints

Prior to starting my own firm, I served as a senior partner at a large consulting firm that worked with financial services companies. The CEO of my firm (who was in from our home office in California) and I made a call on the CEO of the largest bank in North America at that time. When my CEO asked the bank's CEO how much time he had, he smiled slightly and said an hour. About 55 minutes into the call, when my CEO paused and said to the bank CEO, "We have five minutes left to wrap up," the bank CEO smiled broadly and said, "Don't worry about that. Let's go on."

I learned several things from that high level exchange. The first is that everyone is time deprived, and even CEOs can build good will by thanking customers for their time and asking them how much time they have available. The second is that by "checking in" with customers and giving them the chance to end the meeting on or before the allotted time, we deepen rapport. What's interesting is that by signaling them that you respect their time, many customers will actually extend the meeting.

Congratulate Customers

As long as you are sincere, don't hesitate to congratulate customers on some achievement their company or they have been cited for. This might include, for example, strong revenue or profit results for a given quarter or year, or recognition for community service. Examples include being named as one of the most admired companies; having high employee participation in a Red Cross blood drive or a United Way campaign; and sponsoring a scholarship. Or you can congratulate customers for something they personally have achieved, such as winning a golf, bridge, or bowling tournament, writing an article, or giving a talk.

Recently, I was scheduled to meet with the president of a manufacturing company and happened to read in the local paper that he was being honored by the local Red Cross chapter as a Father of the Year. When I congratulated him at our meeting, his stern expression turned into a smile, and we had a great conversation about parenting prior to our business discussion. No doubt, he appreciated the fact that I did a bit of research on him.

Be Reassuring

On a recent sales call on a manufacturing company whose business I had been trying to land for more than a year, I recommended to the vice president of sales that it would be valuable for us to meet with the president of his division. After agreeing to my suggestion, he turned toward me and, referring to the president, said, "I hope Carl does not start wondering why I have not done what you're recommending, Ron." I reassured the vice president by pointing out that, given how much revenues and market share increased on his watch despite a weak economy, the president could not fault him for anything. And the president would likely be impressed by the vice president's feeling confident enough to proactively consider ideas from both internal and external thought-leaders. Sure enough, after our meeting, the president complimented the vice president for seeking out new ideas to help the company build on its success.

Be Empathetic

Whether the salesperson or his company is struggling or not, when a customer says, "I need to think it over," many salespeople ask, "Could you please tell me exactly what you need to think about?" Or, "I can save you some time, if you like, by telling you about the competition and how we are different."

Although that is a reasonable question and can reveal useful information, my experience tells me a better approach is to say, "I don't blame you." Or, "It's an important decision." Or, "Of course, you want to make the right decision." Only then should the salesperson ask, "How can I help you in your decision?" Or, "What else would you like to know to help you make the best decision."

Tell Customers Why You Are There

One of the simplest things you can do to put customers at ease and show you are empathetic is to tell them the purpose of your call. But remember to do so in a way that does not pressure the customer. For example, unless it's been agreed to in advance, don't say: "I'm here to have you sign our contract." Instead, you might say: "I'm here to present our proposal and determine our next steps."

Mirror Your Customers' Body Language

Mirroring customers is good; aping customers is not. Customers like to buy from people they trust, and the truth is most people are more comfortable buying from people like themselves. That is why mirroring customers can be helpful—assuming you don't overdo it. You can mirror customers by adapting your body language, word choice, and vocal quality to reflect theirs, but use good judgment in doing so. For example, if your customer is leaning forward and smiling, you may want to do the same. However, if your customer is leaning back and frowning, of course, you should not follow suit.

Mirroring is most powerful where it is done subtly and where it focuses on word choice, rather than vocal quality. Those who have studied the science of neuro-linguistics report that many people have a predominant language style and use words that are primarily auditory, visual, or kinesthetic. For example, customers who are auditorily dominant may say: "I hear what you're saying," "Listen to me," or "That sounds great." Customers who are visually dominant may say: "See what I mean?" "Here's my vision for the company," or, "From my vantage point." A third group, who are tactile-driven, may use words like: "I can feel it," "Let me get my arms around it," or "We have really been squeezed." Mirroring is most effective when the customer does not know you're doing it. And mirroring their word choice is one of the most powerful ways to make even cautious customers feel comfortable and win them over.

Use Humor

I once built rapport with a customer who had a photo of a catamaran sailboat in his office, through humor. I told him that on my 30th birthday, on an impulse, I bought a used sunfish, but once I got it out in the bay, I always had trouble sailing it back to shore, and one of the happiest days of my life was when my sunfish was stolen! My self-effacing comment got the customer to reveal that he could never get the hang of golf and once shot a 36 for three holes! Of course, your humor should always be inoffensive and in good taste.

What Did You Do for Me Today?

Given how much many business executives have on their plate, it is not sufficient to build rapport once—even if that includes doing them a good deed—because customers may simply forget it. Maintaining rapport is not a one-time event, but an ongoing process, and all salespeople—and especially ones who have not yet hit their revenue goals—need to continuously look for ways to help their customers meet their personal and business needs.

5 More Ways to Build Rapport

Top-performing salespeople build rapport by:

1. Building bridges to customers by mentioning shared connections to their school, neighborhood, hobby, favorite sports team, mutual acquaintance, or other common interest.

2. Being more open to revealing personal interests or experiences that customers may share.

3. Entering the information they know about their customers into their database, so they will instantly have a way of reconnecting with their customers in subsequent discussions.

4. Sending their customers useful information that helps them in their business and personal lives.

5. Showing customers they enjoy being with them by inviting them out to breakfast, lunch, dinner, a sporting event, or theater.

Make Building Rapport Part of Your Business Development Strategy

Whether you are soaring or struggling, be sure to build rapport so that your customers feel more comfortable answering questions and disclosing information critical to a sale. You can put cautious customers at ease when you greet them warmly, exhibit empathy, and employ humor.

Ask Questions to Uncover Reluctant Customers' Needs and Concerns

Top-performing salespeople ask four times as many questions as their-less successful colleagues.

— Ron Volper Group 2010 Sales Study

Not long ago, I had a hacking cough and fever. After a couple of days of misery, I succumbed to my wife's loving, persistent hint-dropping, and dragged myself reluctantly to the doctor. Here's how our discussion went:

Doctor: Hi, Ron. What brings you in to see me today?

Ron: I'm feeling lousy, Doc.

Doctor: Sorry to hear that. What's making you feel lousy?

Ron: I've been coughing a lot for several days.

Doctor: What kind of cough are we talking about?

Ron: Well, my throat hurts when I cough.

Doctor: Is it a dry cough, or do you cough anything up?

Ron: Dry.

Doctor: Okay. Can you tell me how often you're coughing, and during what time of the day you cough?

Ron: Throughout the day and all through the night. I'm having trouble sleeping.

Doctor: Any other symptoms?

Ron: Yes. I've been running a fever.

Doctor: Oh! For how long?

Ron: For about three days.

Doctor: I see. What's the highest it's been?

Ron: It was 101 last night.

Doctor: Is that the last time you checked it?

Ron: Yes.

Doctor: Is anyone else in your family ill?

Ron: No.

Doctor: Have you been around anyone lately who was ill?

Ron: No.

Doctor: I didn't see any indication of allergies on your chart. Do you have any?

Ron: Not that I know of.

Doctor: Have you tried taking anything for your cough or throat?

Ron: No.

Doctor: Okay, why don't you let me examine you now so we can figure out what's going on.

The Information Is There...But You Have to Ask for It

My doctor didn't assume that he had the information he needed to treat me. Only after he had asked me all those questions—and then examined me—did he prescribe a solution. I'm happy to say that I have long since recovered from that cough. But that visit to my doctor got me wondering: Why do so many salespeople assume they have the truth about a prospect or customer's situation and then make a diagnosis without asking enough questions, or the right questions, or *any* questions, up-front?

According to a recent study, young children ask as many as 75 questions a day. That's how they learn about the world and their place in it. Top salespeople are a lot like these kids in that they have an innate curiosity and a desire to know as much as possible about people's needs and wants. Asking good questions not only helps them to identify a potential solution; it also enables them to quickly qualify the account and determine how much time they should invest in it.

Questions: The Secret Weapon

During my first two years in sales—when I knew a whole lot less about my company and its products than I did later on—I sold more than I did in my third year. I eventually discovered one of the reason for this was that, during those first two years, I asked my customers more questions and I learned more about them. My questions were my secret weapon, although I didn't realize that at the time. Many years later, after I established the Ron Volper Group as a national sales consulting firm, my staff and I conducted a number of sales studies that confirmed my own experience about questioning. The studies showed that sales stars ask far more questions than their peers—four times as many.

Not surprisingly, the salespeople who asked better questions, and closed more business, tended to know more about their customers. We asked salespeople in 10 different industries, all of whom had exceeded their revenue goals, to draw an organizational chart of their customers. Roughly 90 percent of salespeople from this group could do so. On the other hand, when we asked salespeople who were behind in their revenue goals to do the same thing, only 40 percent could do so.

Talk Less—Listen More

When salespeople are behind in their numbers, they often do the exact opposite of what works best. Because they are anxious to pump up sales, they start spouting as much information as they can about their company and its products, instead of asking their customers questions about their needs and wants, and listening to the answers. The latter approach is known as *need-based selling,* and questioning is at its core. Because they ask more questions, top salespeople talk less than struggling salespeople do, and they talk later in the call.

Do Pre-Call Research

As head of sales for a Fortune 500 company, one of the most disastrous—and shortest—calls I ever observed was when one of my salespeople asked a customer, "What do you guys do here?" That's the kind of question whose answer you need to know before you walk in the door. Early in my sales career, prior to the advent of the Internet, I often agonized over whether or not I should take the time to run over to the public library in Greenwich, Connecticut, to do research on a company before calling them. Today, with the technological tools we have at our disposal, at a minimum, every salesperson can check the prospect's Website and do other online research before engaging in a discussion. Pre-call research positions you to ask cautious customers better questions, and thus adds to your credibility. Social media sites such as LinkedIn and Facebook can be helpful in finding friends and colleagues who may know something about the customer.

Use a *O-N-E Strategy* to Ask Better Questions

I use what I call the *O-N-E Strategy* to facilitate better questions. Once I increased the number and quality of my questions, my appointments and my sales increased. A better question is one that:

» Reveals valuable customer information and customer needs that is not available elsewhere.

» Flows logically from the previous question.

» Engages customers and does not make them uncomfortable.

Orientation Questions

These questions are "big picture" questions about the industry and the company's history, mission, vision, values, goals, and challenges. Orientation Questions are based on information learned about the company from pre-call research. For example, I have asked customers: "I read that your company announced that it is preparing to go public. How do you foresee that changing the way you manage the sales and marketing function?"

Needs-Based Questions

These are questions about specific problems or opportunities the company faces that my firm may be able to help with. What top salespeople do in this area is something that most other salespeople often overlook: They ask questions not only about a company's needs, but also about "the need behind the need." That is, they dig down to find out what is causing the stated need and what makes it important. For example, when a customer of mine told me that it was important that the sales training seminar I was going to conduct be well-received, my first instinct was to say, "Of course." But instead of assuming I knew the reason for her comment, I said the following: "I can understand that. And all my clients want me to conduct an outstanding seminar, but beyond the obvious reasons, is there any other reason why this seminar is important to you?" She responded, "The new CEO of the holding company of which my company is a division will be attending our sales meeting. And this is also my first company-wide meeting as the new VP of sales." Those were important facts for me to know.

My customer's response suggests another benefit of asking needs-based questions. Many buying decisions are made based on personal needs as well as organizational needs, so it's important for the salesperson to uncover the individual perspective as well. If you phrase your question tactfully, it's appropriate for you to ask your prospect or customer how solving or not solving a company problem will personally affect him or her. So, in response to the comment from the VP of sales that this was to be her first company-wide meeting with the sales team, I asked, "How will it help you personally if the sales seminar and the meeting are successful?"

Effect Questions

These are questions about how eliminating a problem mentioned or maximizing an opportunity can help the organizations and individuals achieve their goals. Effect Questions can be thought of as "sad and glad" questions. These questions get the prospect or customer to think about the (sad) consequences of *not* taking action on a need for your product, or conversely, about the benefit of solving that need (which, of course, would make the customer feel glad).

Most salespeople stop at needs-based questions, and many salespeople don't even get that far, but simply present their product without asking any meaningful questions at all. Our research, however, indicates that top salespeople not only ask more questions overall, but ask roughly five times as many Effect Questions as other salespeople. It is not sufficient for the salespeople to ask "What effect does X have on your company?" They go further. For example, if the prospect says "By not fixing that problem we lose revenue," a star salesperson might ask "Approximately how much revenue would you say you are losing annually?"

Open-Ended Questions

Top sales professionals ask many different types of questions, but it's worth noticing that they usually ask three times as many *open-ended questions* as their less-successful peers. Open-ended questions are those that require a more extended response than a simple yes or no, and often elicit feelings as well as facts. One benefit of asking open-ended questions is that they can make customers feel relaxed, and relaxed customers often tell you more about their needs.

There are potential downsides to asking open-ended questions: They are more difficult to think of than closed-ended questions, and the salesperson who asks them runs the risk of losing control of the conversation. Yet conducting a sales conversation that relies exclusively on closed-ended yes or no questions is far riskier.

Closed-Ended Questions

Closed-ended questions can be answered with a yes or no response, or with a brief, usually factual response. For example, "Where were you born?" is a closed-ended question, whereas "What was it like growing up in Chicago?" is an open-ended question. Another example of a closed-ended question is "How long have you been with your company?" "What's it like working at your company?" is an open-ended question. See the difference? One benefit of closed-ended questions is that they help you control the sales call by guiding the direction of the conversation. Asking too many of them, however, can leave the cautious customer feeling as though you've launched an interrogation.

Silence Is a Powerful Information-Gathering Tool

You may have heard the sales expression "The first one who talks loses." Well, it's wrong. If the customer talks first, both you and the customer win, because by telling you about their needs, customers give you an opportunity to satisfy them. Many customers just need a few seconds of silence to expand on what they've already told you, or to share something new.

Statement Questions

A third type of question that can enhance the call for any salesperson is the Statement Question. This is simply a statement that is followed by a brief pause that invites the customer to contribute an opinion or insight. For example, you might say "Many people I know loved growing up in your hometown." Most people would respond to this statement question by offering additional information.

Ask to Ask

Another strategy top-performing salespeople use to make their questions seem less intrusive is to ask permission to ask questions, and mention the benefits of their doing so. Anyone can use this approach to disarm customers and get them to open up. For example, I sometimes ask "Would you mind if I ask you some questions to help us both determine whether and how we might be able to accelerate the revenues of your company?"

The Power of Paper

Another approach that works for me in eliciting information from less-talkative people is to hand them a document and ask them to comment on it. For example, in talking with C-level executives about how sales-driven their company is (or isn't), I realized that some of them simply did not want to spend their time thinking about the issue. So instead of asking them about it, I started handing them a graphic summarizing my firm's research on the characteristics of sales-driven companies; I then asked them to comment on which sales drivers their company was strong in.

Ask Questions With a Light Touch

Early in my sales career, I was trying to gather as much information as possible from an executive vice president at a major bank. I must have been barraging him with too many questions that were too abrupt, for he turned to me at one point and said, "Son, are you trying to find problems?" Needless to say, I did not get his business, but I did learn a valuable lesson: Not only do I need to gather as much information as possible, but I need to do it deftly, and make the conversation a pleasant experience for my customer.

Ask for Clarification

Another important guideline to follow when it comes to keeping things light is to ask for clarification before you jump to conclusions about your prospect's intentions. Let's say you've been working on a large, complex sale (one with many moving parts and lots of coalition-building involving multiple stakeholders). Let's also say that, after working on this account for months, your contact, who had promised you that you were now the sole vendor, led off your face-to-face meeting with this statement: "I wanted you to know that, based on the most recent draft of your proposal, we're going to need to start reaching out to some other suppliers."

Any variation of "How could you do this to me?" is not using a light touch! On the other hand, if you were to ask for guidance in understanding what part of the proposal your contact was talking about, and what "reaching out to other suppliers" really means, you could keep the dialogue alive, and gather the information you need. It's possible, for example, that there's simply a problem with a delivery date on a specific product, and that your contact is planning to get a quote on this (tiny) portion of the overall deal—unless you can improve the schedule.

Using a light touch also means sending the right verbal supports during the conversation. Let the customer know you are listening by offering support statements such as, ""I see," "That's interesting," or even "Uh-huh." And, of course, you should always try to maintain appropriate eye contact.

A Quip Can Get a Laugh

One of the best ways to make the interaction more pleasant for your customer is to inject humor into your questions. Obviously, your humor should be tasteful and appropriate. For example, in a recent meeting with the new vice president of sales at a Fortune 500 company, I began the discussion by congratulating him on his appointment, then, with tongue in cheek, said, "We both know managing salespeople can be challenging. What's your approach to managing the loveable prima donnas who are on your team?" He smiled and started telling stories. That's always a good sign.

8 Ways to Improve Questions and Jump-Start Sales

1. Write out the most essential information you would like to uncover about the company and its needs.

2. Jot down approximately 10 questions to elicit this information. Then put an asterisk next to the five most important ones.

3. After building rapport with the customer, tell her you would like to ask her some questions so that you can make the best recommendations to raise her sales.

4. Incorporate some of what you have learned in your up-front research into the wording of your questions. For example, "I read that your company made an offer to acquire one of your competitors. What impact might that have on your marketing and sales objectives?"

5. Start with open-ended questions and then gather more detailed information by asking more closed-ended questions.

6. Use Statement Questions, especially with customers who are more cautious and less talkative.

7. Remember that silence also often works as a great "question."

8. Use complimentary questions rather than critical ones, especially early in the call.

Responding to Your Customer's Questions

One important and often overlooked issue about questions has to do with how to respond when the customer starts questioning you. As a general rule, questions from customers are positive signs, because they suggest that the other person is interested in learning more about your company and your products. There are, however, two big risks you run in responding to customer questions. First, you may fail to answer the question clearly or to the cautious customer's satisfaction. And, second, you may lose control of the conversation and fail to obtain the information you need to make a sale.

Before responding to customers' questions, I recommend you do the following: thank them for the question; then, if you are at all unsure about what the question is trying to uncover, ask a clarifying question; finally, answer the question to the best of your knowledge. In order not to lose control of the conversation, I also recommend that you answer the customers' questions briefly and then immediately follow up with a question of your own. The only exception to this rule is that if you are talking to customers with high-control needs (and many CEOs fall into this category), you should usually answer all their questions before posing your own.

Being a Professional Salesperson Is a Lot Like Being a Detective

Salespeople, like detectives, need to ferret out critical information if they are going to be successful. That's why asking questions plays such a critical role in the sales process and why the most successful salespeople know not only what questions to ask, but when and how to ask them.

Strategy 4

Offer Recommendations to Curb Cautious Customers' Fears

More business is lost not from too high a price, but because over-eager salespeople pitch their products before they fully understand the needs of their customers.
—Ron Volper Group 2010 Sales Study

During the American Revolutionary War, General Israel Putnam told his troops fighting the British soldiers, "Hold your fire until you see the whites of their eyes." In their eagerness to make a sale, a common mistake that struggling salespeople make is that they "shoot from the lip" by firing off information about their product or service before they have fully uncovered their customers' needs and assessed their motivation to finding a solution. A sale can slip out of your hands if you toss out a recommendation too soon, so "hold your fire" and first gather all the facts.

Involve Your Customers in the Sales Process

Although most of today's customers are cautious out of necessity, they are more likely to buy from you if you first demonstrate that you fully understand what they need before offering any recommendations. This is accomplished by involving customers in not only defining the problem, but, where feasible, in crafting the recommendations. Although the customer will not know your products as well as you do, you honor customers by inviting them to participate in thinking through two or three options with you, and then offering your recommendation.

For example, instead of sounding pushy by telling your customer, "Here's what you should do..." you will encourage his "buy in" if you say something like, "I see two possible options that may help you take advantage of that opportunity (or address that problem). Let's discuss them and together we can figure out which would work best for you."

Benefits Are in the Eye of the Customer

Would you even consider buying a one-size-fits-all suit or outfit? Probably not. Yet this is a common mistake new salespeople often make when attempting to define the features and benefits of their products or services to customers during sales calls. They assume every feature is a benefit for every customer. However, even before understanding how to convert features into benefits that meet the needs of your customer, it's important to differentiate between a product or service's features and benefits.

A *feature* is a fact about your product or service, whereas a benefit is how that feature meets a specific customer need. Top salespeople know that customers buy products and services because of their benefits—not because of their features. Benefits enable organizations, businesses, and individuals to save time, money, and effort, be more profitable, eliminate waste, and do what they do more efficiently.

For example, a savvy computer salesperson could differentiate between the features and benefits this way: "This powerful laptop computer features six gigabytes of RAM, weighs only 1.5 pounds, and has a 15-inch screen. The benefits of these features are that it can run several software programs simultaneously, which saves you time. It's also totally portable and the large screen is easy on the eyes."

Apply the "So What?" Test

Top-performing salespeople also know that not all the benefits of a product or service—no matter how fancy or useful they may be—appeal equally to all customers. So how do you know which of your product or services' features can become benefits that meet the needs of your customer? The answer is to apply the "So what?" test.

Let's say you're a salesperson at a new car dealership and the car you offer comes in burgundy, blue, or beige. If the customer does not like any of these three colors, he may be thinking "So what?" and will not see those colors as a benefit. In fact, the color choice may even create a reason not to buy the car. Similarly, let's say that, because of the manufacturer's use of a new composite material, the car you're selling weighs less than other models and therefore gets better gas mileage. Many salespeople would probably cite fuel savings as a benefit, but you'd be running a small risk in mentioning that, unless during the course of your discussion, the customer expressed a need for reducing fuel costs.

Though many customers may have that need, not all would agree that it is as important as some other benefits. Some customers might think, "Yes, but in the event of an accident a lightweight car will not protect me as well as a heavier one, and the ride will not be as comfortable." Even if the customer does see reducing fuel costs as a need, he or she may see it as a "nice to have" rather than a "must have." Therefore, it is best not to emphasize particular benefits until you have prioritized the customer's needs. Then when the customer asks, "So what?" the answer will clearly identify that the benefit is important enough to justify the purchase.

Measuring the Impact of Action and Inaction

Many inexperienced or struggling salespeople often pitch their products or services without suggesting what impact they may have on their customer's profitability. On the other hand, top salespeople focus first on their product's "value proposition" because businesses will usually not invest in a product or service unless they can see a potential return on their investment. In order to do that, you need to understand how satisfying specific needs will help the customer's bottom line and ideally help your customer personally.

"What Is the Cost of Doing Nothing?"

For cautious customers to make a change—especially one that involves an expensive purchase—top salespeople will first walk them through a measuring process that focuses on the cost of doing nothing. For example, let's say that the XYZ Widget Company's manufacturing plant turns out 100 widgets per month and sells each widget for $1,000. However, because they are using an outdated machine and inefficient process, 10 percent of the units they produce per month are defective and must be discarded. Without being heavy-handed, to focus on the cost of your customer doing nothing, you might ask: "With your current widget machine, you've told me that you lose 10 units a month due to defects. If they were not defective, these 10 units could sell for $1,000 each, so your monthly loss in sales revenue due to defective widgets is $10,000. Is that about right?"

I might then proceed to tally indirect costs, such as the time involved in replacing these defective units and, more importantly, the ill will they create with customers, and the possible loss of referrals from dissatisfied customers.

Describe a Potential Return on Investment

Once you and your customer have defined how much it costs not to change, the time is right to describe your product or service's value proposition and potential return on investment. However, struggling salespeople who make promises they can't legitimately support reflects not only their desperation, but a lack of experience and credibility. That's why your chances of convincing a prospect to consider buying your products or services will improve if you describe *potential* returns on a given investment or related case studies that support your claims. For example, you could say, "Okay, we've determined that you're losing $10,000 a month due to this old machine of yours cranking out defective units. Let me ask you this: If I could walk you through how one of my other clients with a similar situation used a more efficient widget machine to increase their profits, would you be interested in hearing more?"

Describe Benefits in Terms of Increasing Positive Outcomes and Decreasing Negative Situations

Even cautious customers will be more open to your recommendations if you demonstrate a return on their investment by using the terms *increase* and *decrease* in discussing benefits. For example, you might say, "Would you be interested in letting me show you how we can *increase* your company's profits (revenue, efficiency, image, product quality, customer referrals, customer satisfaction, market share, staff morale and retention, and so on)?" Or, "Would you be interested in letting me show you how we can *decrease* your company's cost of raw materials (customer churn, dependence on vendors, government penalties, hiring missteps, litigation issues, loss of talent to your competitors, management/staff conflict, order fulfillment time, product defects, production and marketing costs, staff complaints, waste of resources and time, and so on)?"

Make Recommendations Where Your Competition Fails to Meet Your Customers' Needs

In today's global economy, it's common to encounter both local and foreign competitors in a major sale. However, struggling salespeople in their eagerness to make a sale sometimes forget to prepare for challenges from all their competitors. With a few computer keystrokes, it's easy to learn about your competition from online sources, from company files, and sometimes even from shopping the competition. And top salespeople know that the most useful information about your competition can come from your customers. Here's how you can tap into this goldmine of "business intelligence."

When you ask you customers during a sales call if they are talking to other companies, they often will tell you what you want to know. Most top-performing salespeople know that running down their competition to their customers can have the opposite effect on the sale, so instead they gently ask questions about their competitors' offers or products. As result, they learn a great deal of information that can help differentiate them from their competitors.

In addition, I've noticed that when I ask prospects what they like about my competitors, they tell me, and then, without further prompting, often go on to reveal what they dislike about them. This business intelligence can help you point out your products' benefits without directly referring to your competitors. At the same time, whether customers have decided in your favor or not, you can also attempt to get them to disclose what they like and dislike about your product or service versus your competitors."

Take Your Time and Make More Sales

If your specific market is down and you are struggling to make your numbers, you may be tempted to rush your sales pitch, especially with busy or cautious customers. However, before you cut to the bottom line and quote a price, take a step back and consider why customers will buy from you in the first place. If you take the time to define their needs and target specific benefits of your product or service to address their needs, they will know that you've listened. And, if instead of promising an unsubstantiated "solution," you engage in a collaborative discussion of options—including doing nothing—and then describe potential returns on investments for your recommendation, you'll gain credibility with your customers. The ultimate result of this approach? The more time you take to fully understand your customers' needs and offer the best recommendations with the highest return on investment, the greater the likelihood that you will make the sale, and turn your customers into advocates for your company.

Strategy 5

Address Objections to Persuade Risk-Adverse Customers

Seventy percent of salespeople said they failed to close business because of price, whereas only 45 percent of their customers said price was their main objection.
—Ron Volper Group 2010 Sales Study

I got angry early in my sales career when customers raised objections to my proposed solutions, especially during a month when my sales numbers were down. I became even more rattled when my sales manager (who had never been a salesperson himself) once chided me by saying, "Ron, if you do a good job on the call, customers won't ever have any objections."

I was wrong to get angry, but my manager was even more wrong in his belief that objections are a bad thing. In fact, objections are often a positive step in the sales cycle, because they suggest that customers have been listening and mulling over the pros and cons of our proposed solutions.

In some cases, customers may be intent on purchasing our products, but are simply raising objections in an attempt to get us to lower our price. The classic example is that many people, while negotiating the price of a used car, will point out its flaws in an attempt to get sellers to reduce the price. Top-performing salespeople sometimes say that a sales call was too easy. What they mean is that if customers voice no objections, they are probably not seriously considering their product or service. The real selling begins when the objections start flowing.

Surfacing Objections

One mistake that struggling salespeople make is to ignore their customers' objections. As a result, they either give up on making the sale or try to pressure the customer into making a commitment. Star salespeople do just the opposite. They listen for even hints of objections, and encourage their customer to express them. If you don't, you have not removed the objections from your customer's mind, and though you may have moved on to another issue, your customer may still be stuck on it and not paying attention to anything else you say.

If you do sense a customer concern, rather than saying, "You seem to have an objection," take the emotion out of it by not using the word *objection,* and saying something like: "I may be mistaken, Mr. Customer, but you seem to have a question." This will make your customer feel more comfortable sharing what's on his mind.

The Ron Volper Group conducted a survey in which we asked salespeople in a range of industries why they did not succeed in closing a piece of business. In 70 percent of the cases, salespeople attributed their lost business to price. We then went back and asked these customers why they did not buy from that salesperson. Although "too high a price" was still the most common reason for not buying according to the customers, it was the main factor in only 45 percent of cases. Some of the other reasons customers cited were that they:

> Did not perceive a need.

> Didn't like the company.

> Felt another company's product more closely met their needs.

› Didn't feel comfortable with the salesperson.

› Had a relationship with another company or salesperson.

› Found the presentation or proposal disappointing.

› Decided to use an in-house solution.

› Did not have time to think about it or implement the product.

Once customers reveal their objections I recommend using the following five-step process:

Step 1: Thank them for sharing their concerns.

Step 2: Paraphrase what they told you to be sure you understand their objections correctly.

Step 3: Before answering the specific objection, ask customers if they have any other objections. This question gets all their objections out on the table at once and prevents customers from trapping you in a never-ending game of objections and answers.

Step 4: Once your customers have described all their concerns, then ask specific questions about particular objections. One reason to do this is to understand exactly what they mean by certain words, such as "Your price it too high."

The message here is clear: If customers express a concern about price (or anything else), rather than immediately respond, first ask them to describe their concern about your price more specifically. For example, you might ask:

» "Is the real issue your price or your budget?"

» "How does my price compare to the other company's price?"

» "Is my current price more than what you've previously paid?"

> » "For you to agree to this price, do you need someone else's approval?"

> » "Do you feel that our price is worth what you'll get for it?"

Step 5:   As you answer each objection, check with your customers to be sure that they are satisfied with your response.

Using this five-step process demonstrates a respect for your customers, and by delaying your response until you have more information, you give yourself more time to frame a more thoughtful response. However, the biggest payoff for you is that it increases the likelihood of making the sales process one in which your customers will view you as a partner (and a thought leader) rather than as an adversary trying to force-fit a product on them.

Maintain Your Professional Presence While Dealing With Objections

Besides using the process just described to overcome objections, you need to maintain your professional presence in responding to objections. That means maintaining your composure and sounding consultative rather than defensive in what you say and how you say it. Part of professional presence means that you demonstrate empathy for the customer. For example, if the customer says, "This is a big decision and we want to get it right," don't respond with false assurances or platitudes. Instead, say something such as: "I understand. My goal is to make sure all the details are correct and that you are happy with the result."

Responding to Objections and Obstacles

The way you convince a hesitant customer to agree to a sale depends upon the type of concerns he or she has. Customer concerns generally fall into two categories: objections and obstacles.

Objections are based on needs customers have that they believe—correctly or incorrectly—that your company's product or service cannot satisfy. There are three main types of objections, and you should use a different strategy in responding to each.

Objections Based on Misunderstandings

The first type of objection is a *misunderstanding*. In this case, customers have incorrect information, but do not realize it. They may have misinterpreted something you or someone else said, did not correctly recall the information, or read or heard something that was at one time true, but is no longer correct or valid. For example, if a customer tells her banker that she is moving her account to another bank because she needs a bank that has evening hours and, in fact, your bank does have evening hours, the customer is voicing a misunderstanding.

In handling a misunderstanding, accept the responsibility for the customer's confusion or inaccurate information, even if you are not to blame. You can clarify your customer's view by saying something like, "I'm sorry if I was not clear. I'm happy to tell you that our branch right near you is open until 8 p.m. on Thursday evenings."

Objections Based on Doubt

The second type of objection is based on a *doubt*. In this case, the customer does not accept what you are saying. Here you need to offer some form of proof. Not necessarily proof that would stand up in a court of law, but enough proof that will eliminate the customer's doubt. For example, if a customer does not believe that your bank pays one of the highest rates of interest on a certificate of deposit, you might show them the results of a survey from an independent source comparing bank interest rates.

Objections Based on Drawbacks

The third type of objection is based on a *drawback*. Here, the customer has a need that your product cannot satisfy. For example, if customers want the automobile you are selling in green and it only comes in red, blue, or black, this represents a drawback for those customers. You can use one of two strategies to overcome a drawback. You can outweigh the objection by reminding customers of other benefits of the product. (Remember that a benefit is a customer need that your product *can* satisfy.) Or you can suggest an alternative.

In the first instance, you might say, "Though it's true we do not offer the car in green, you did mention, Ms. Customer, that you liked the excellent gas mileage and the comfortable handling of our car. Doesn't that more than compensate for not having your first choice of color?" The other option is to offer alternatives, by saying something like, "Although it's not available in green, many of our customers think the car looks great in blue. Let's take a look at one." One caveat when you offer customers alternatives is to not confuse them by suggesting too many options.

Responding to Obstacles

Obstacles are concerns that do not relate to your product or company, but rather to customers' internal matters. For instance, if a customer wants to enter into a contract to purchase a home but requires a spouse's signature, the real estate salesperson might ask the customer when his or her the spouse will be able to sign it. To increase the odds of closing the sale with at least one of the pair, the salesperson could ask alternatively, "If you could make the decision yourself, would you be in favor of buying the property?"

Obstacles vs. Excuses

Asking questions not only surfaces the real concern, but tells you whether the customer faces a real obstacle to buying your product or whether he is simply giving you an excuse. An excuse, or *stall,* often means that the customer has no need for or interest in your product or service, but for any one of a number of reasons thinks it's easier to fabricate a reason why he or she can't buy from you. For example, for those customers who really do make it a practice to check with their spouse before making a decision, not having done so is a valid obstacle. If, on the other hand, the customer is just saying this, or may not even have a spouse, then this is a classic excuse.

I once joined an inexperienced salesperson on a call to the senior vice president of marketing at a global hotel company. As the salesperson presented his recommendations, it was clear from the SVP's body language and the lack of questions that he was not overly enamored with the salesperson's proposal. At the end of the call, when the salesperson asked the SVP if he would like to move ahead with implementation of his recommended services, the SVP said he could not do so without the concurrence of the vice president (who reported to him!), and the vice president was out on maternity leave for three months. In this case, it was clear to me (but unfortunately not to the salesperson) that this was an excuse, rather than a genuine obstacle.

Useful Information Is the Best Remedy for Selling More in a Down Market

Useful information for you and your customer can make the difference between closing and losing a sale. The more you probe into your customers' obstacles, the more opportunities you have to offer possible solutions. For example, in the previous case, you might ask the SVP with the absent VP:

> "What other concerns do you have?"

> "Is your VP available to review or discuss the proposal on a conference call?"

> "I'm happy to e-mail the proposal to her, if that would help."

> "I'm curious: How has your company made other decisions in the VP's absence?"

You can also distinguish between an excuse and an obstacle by asking open-ended or closed-ended questions, or by using a Statement Question. For example, if you suspect that the customer is not being truthful with you, you might say, something like, "Sometimes customers tell me that when they are not really interested in our product but don't want to hurt my feelings." And then wait for the customer to respond.

Similarly, some customers will say, "Let me think about it." This statement may be valid or it may be an excuse. But in either case, you need to ask more questions to determine what the customer really means.

When struggling salespeople hear a prospect say, "Let me think about it," they may respond, "When should I check back with you?" Although that's a polite response, it ends the sales process, at least for the time being. On the other hand, star salespeople are more likely to say something such as, "I can understand that this is an important decision for you. Perhaps, I can save you some time. May I ask what are some of the things you will be thinking about in making this decision?"; "Will you be conferring with anyone else on this decision?"; or "Just for the sake of discussion, if you were making a decision at this time, which way are you leaning?"

A similar customer comment that may be an obstacle but is more likely an excuse is "I now have too much on my plate. Give me a call in two or three months." Again, it's conceivable that the customer, especially if he or she is a senior executive, is extremely busy, but it's equally likely that the customer is making an excuse. For that reason, gently probe to find out the real meaning behind the comment. For example, you might say, "Ms. Customer, without asking you to reveal any confidential information, may I ask you what will be different for you in two or three months?" If the customer simply says she is very busy at this time, there's a good chance this is not the real reason.

Practice Responding to Common Objections

When it comes to objections, the good news is that most salespeople hear the same objections (particularly about price) over and over. Therefore, one easy and fast way to boost your sales is to write these common objections down in a notebook. Then come up with some reasonable solutions that address your customers' concerns. Practice your responses and try them out on your customers to see how convincing they are. You can make this activity even more useful by doing it with one or more colleagues. That way you'll be ready with smart answers to overcome the most common reasons why your customers don't buy.

Strategy 6 — Gain Hesitant Customers' Commitment

There is no correlation between the type of close salespeople use and their success in getting customers to commit to a next step.

—Ron Volper Group 2010 Sales Study

Recently, I was asked by the CEO of a well-known insurance company my firm had not previously done business with to give a talk on how to close sales at their annual meeting. I agreed to his request on the spot. However, as I was preparing my talk, a troubling thought popped into my mind. I wondered why he was asking me to talk about closing skills as opposed to any other sales topic. So I picked up the phone and asked him that question. His response was that his team's new business was down from the previous year. After further discussion and some joint calls with his salespeople, it became clear to me that rather than closing skills, his team really needed "opening skills."

That is, his sales team had a high conversion rate (the ratio of accounts in the pipeline that they closed), but they were not adequately prospecting for new accounts and putting enough of them in the pipeline. Their difficulty in bringing in new business was not related to a weakness in closing skills, but rather to their difficulty in getting appointments. After reviewing my findings, the CEO, to his credit, heard what I said and agreed that my talk should be about developing new business, rather than closing skills.

How Closing Helps Customers

That said, salespeople who have not yet reached their sales goals close less often on sales calls and *are* often less adept at closing than their peers who have exceeded their goals. Closing is beneficial for customers, as well as salespeople. The act of closing can be thought of the way inviting a friend over to your home for dinner can: After the friend has accepted your invitation and arrived at your home, it is up to you as the host (not your friend) to decide when dinner is served, and to invite your friend to sit down and eat.

If you ever have any hesitation about closing, ask yourself this question: After customers make time to see you, and invite you to come to their office, do you really think your customers would be surprised if you as a salesperson were to invite them to take the next step in the sales process?

5 Reasons Closing Fails

My firm's research and my own experience suggest that there are five reasons why salespeople have trouble closing a customer.

1. Salespeople who are not where they want to be put too much pressure on their customers—and themselves—by closing prematurely. They worry so much about the outcome of the call that they don't relax, ask enough questions, or listen for their customers' needs. There is a popular belief in sales that says "ABC—Always Be Closing." It sounds good, but it's not true and it causes a lot of salespeople to alienate their customers.

2. Salespeople sometimes talk too much and, as a result, miss customer signals indicating that they are ready to take the next step.

3. If salespeople's closing techniques are clumsy, it erodes customers' confidence in their recommendations and the customers' willingness to commit to a next step.

4. Salespeople have not planned a secondary call objective—so that, if the customer does not commit to the primary call objective, salespeople can offer a secondary objective, which still advances the sale.

5. Salespeople have not yet achieved their sales objectives, are reluctant, or simply fail to ask the customer to take the next step.

Set a Call Objective

It's important to remember that closing does not always mean having the customer sign on the dotted line. For a complex sale (one where there may be many decision-influencers, a number of decision criteria, and many key events before the sale is consummated), the close can be a meaningful step toward the sale. It moves the sale along because it requires client commitment. Whether or not they reach it, star salespeople think through a call objective for every call they make. For example, their call objective might be having the customer commit to:

» Arrange a meeting with the decision-maker.

» Send you a request for proposal.

» Tell you their decision criteria and decision-making process.

» Invite you to deliver a presentation.

» Agree to meet to review your proposal.

» Go on a site tour (for a hotel).

» Contact your references.

» Use your product or service on a pilot or trial basis.

» Send the contract to their legal department.

» Sign a letter of commitment.

» Sign your contract.

» Send you a deposit or a purchase order.

Use *C-A-R-S* to Create Your Call Objective

Top salespeople don't always achieve their call objectives, but they usually have at least one. Good call objectives meet the criteria in the acronym *C-A-R-S*:

C = Customer-Focused

This requires that the customer, not just the salesperson, take some action. For example, the managing director of a federal credit union once asked me to mail him our proposal. Rather than agree to his request, I suggested that we set a time for me to come in and review it with him in person. Only when he agreed to do that, did I agree to write the proposal.

A= Advances the Sale

This means that the customer needs to agree to a step that actually moves you toward a culmination of the sale (for example, you receive payment for your product or service). In most business-to-business sales, it's unrealistic to expect the customer to sign a contract on the first call, but, as mentioned, the salesperson needs to ask the customer to at least commit to a step in that direction.

R = Realistic

It's understandable that salespeople who are often under intense pressure would like all first calls to end with a signed contract or a check in their hands. In a complex sale, that's seldom the case, and especially not when you are trying to win over cautious customers in a down market. Though call objectives should be ambitious, they also need to be realistic.

S = Specific

By specific I mean measurable. If the customer in the previous example agrees to meet with me at some undetermined time, that's positive, but what's better is if he agrees to set a specific time for the meeting.

Set a Secondary Objective

Unlike their peers, top-earning salespeople also set a secondary call objective. In this way, if they are unable to achieve their primary objective (which is usually more ambitious), they can still move the sale along. And if the customer fails to agree to both the primary and the secondary objectives, the salesperson can decide whether or not the sale is worth pursuing.

For example, the salesperson may ask the customer to sign the contract, and the customer might say he needs to first run it by his boss. A top-producing salesperson would have anticipated this possibility before the call, and might recommend that the contact schedule a meeting with the boss for the three of them to review the contract. And if the contact is unwilling to do this, the salesperson will find out exactly why, and decide whether or not the account is still worth pursuing.

Recognize Buying Signals

Besides knowing how to close, top sales professionals are better in knowing when to close. They recognize verbal and non-verbal buying signals, and when the time is opportune to ask customers for commitment. Buying signals in a tough economy may be more subtle because the customer may be more skittish about making a decision and more worried about making the wrong one. For this reason, it is important to stay attuned to changes that suggest that the customer is ready to move to the next step.

Customers in each industry signal their intent to buy from you with different terminology and in different ways. However, there are certain generic indicators that you should always look for. They may be verbal or non-verbal, or they may consist of certain actions customers take. Customers signal they are ready to take the next step by saying things such as:

» "That sounds great."

» "So what's the next step?"

» "When can we get started?"

» "When would I receive it?"

» "Who would actually be performing the service?"

» "What are the payment terms?"

» "Do you take credit cards, electronic payments, or a purchase order?"

» "What is your credit policy?"

» "How long will it take you to complete the project?"

Customers also signal their intent to buy through non-verbal signals (body language), such as:

» Smiling.

» Nodding.

» Unfolding their arms and leaning forward.

» Reaching out to shake your hand.

» Speaking louder or in a more animated fashion.

Finally, customers may signal their intent to buy by taking the following actions:

» Inviting you to join them for breakfast, lunch, or dinner, or a drink.

» Introducing you to others in their company.

» Giving you literature about their company.

» Inviting you to a company function, such as a golf outing.

Whenever you pick up a verbal or non-verbal signal or see a customer taking an action as listed here, recommend the next step, using one of the following closing techniques.

5 Closing Techniques to Up Your Sales

It's important that you plan a call objective and that you attempt to close each call whenever possible. It's less important what type of close you use. However, I do recommend that you use a close that meets two criteria: The first and most important is that the customer will be comfortable with it; the second is that you are comfortable using it. If you are not yet where you want to be—and even if you are—try using each of these closing techniques to see which ones you are most comfortable with.

1. **Assumptive Close**. The salesperson assumes the sale. She tells rather than asks the customer to take the next step. For example, "I'll go ahead and write up the contract for you to sign." This closing technique may work best with a client who is indecisive or does not have high control needs.

2. **Choice Close.** The salesperson offers two positive alternatives. For example, "Would you like me to e-mail you the contract or overnight it to you?" This closing technique often works best with a customer with a slightly higher need for control than in the assumptive close. Note: With this closing technique, never say, "Would you like to go ahead or not?" because you are offering the customer an opportunity to say no.

3. **Direct Ask Close.** The salesperson asks, "Shall I go ahead and write up the contract for you?" This closing technique may work best with a client who has a high need for control, which is the case with many CEOs.

4. **Summary Close.** The salesperson summarizes the key needs and the benefits and then asks for the order. For example, he might say, "You've said that you need a product that enables you to do X, Y and Z, and you've seen how well our product does that." This closing technique often works best with customers who are very analytical.

5. **Urgency Close.** The salesperson mentions that time is of the essence. She might say, for example, "We usually have a price increase at around this time, and I would hate for you to miss out on the current low price." This closing technique works best if what you say is actually true; otherwise you risk eroding your credibility with the customer.

Of course, you can use any one of these closes in combination. For example, you can summarize benefits and then use a Choice Close or an Urgency Close.

Establish Professional Presence

Regardless of the type of closing technique you use, it's important that you convey a sense of confidence and professionalism in your manner and tone of voice. Besides establishing professional presence with your manner and tone of voice, you reinforce your professionalism by discussing with customers, if you have not done so previously, how they will measure the results of your product or service. If they are not prepared to answer this question, you should be prepared to suggest some ways for them to do so.

When Customers Say No

Regardless of which closing technique you use, as long as you're in sales, you'll encounter some customers who will reject your close. Salespeople who are in a slump sometimes make two fundamental mistakes when they hear no. First, they take it personally. They beat up on themselves and assume they did something wrong. In most cases, they've done nothing wrong. It is important to remember, if a customer declines your recommendation, that she is not rejecting you personally. I've often told myself, and salespeople I've worked with, "Don't flatter yourself into thinking the customer is rejecting you. The customer is not even thinking about you. More likely he's thinking about his budget or what his boss will say if he spends the money. What distinguishes star salespeople is that to them no means 'not now,' rather than 'never.'"

The second mistake salespeople make when their close is not accepted is that they forget to ask the customer "why?" Strategy 3 of Overcoming Objections describes various strategies for overcoming objections, but the key point is to identify the specific reason for the objection; try to overcome it; and then ask the customer for commitment a second time.

Unless you uncover a new objection, if the customer still declines to act, you should usually not attempt to close the sale a third time at that meeting. You should, however, revisit it with the customer at another point in time.

Concluding the Call

Sometimes once they close a deal, salespeople who are behind in their numbers forget to conclude the call. That's a mistake. It's important not only to close the sale, but to conclude the call. Recognizing that customers sometimes have second thoughts about their decision, remember to thank them and reassure them about the benefits of their decision—before "buyer's remorse" sets in. For example, you might say: "We are excited about working with you on this project and, based on having done this with many other companies like yours, we are confident that you will see a significant increase in revenues (or profitability, or efficiency, or customer retention) as a result of our partnership with your company."

You can save yourself and your customer time by confirming next steps and time frames at the meeting when the customer says yes, rather than waiting until you're back at your office to contact the customer again. Also encourage customers to ask you any questions they may have and answer them as specifically as you can at that meeting. Before you leave, shake hands, smile, and establish eye contact with the customer. And on the way out, remember to thank the customer's assistant.

When you do return to your office, it's a good idea to send the customer a handwritten note (on your personalized note card) thanking him or her for the business and expressing confidence in the value of your product. Whenever possible, also invite the customer to some celebratory event, such as a luncheon or dinner, golf outing, or ball game. Finally, if you're not the senior person in your company, and especially if it's a good-sized piece of business you've closed, have your company's CEO or C-level executive call the customer's company's decision-maker or CEO to thank him or her for the business and reassure him or her about the anticipated results.

Give Sales Presentations That Win Over Anxious Customers

Top salespeople write out and practice their sales presentations three times more often than less successful salespeople.
—Ron Volper Group 2010 Sales Study

Early in my sales career, I was locked in a struggle against two larger and better-known competitors for a six-figure sales consulting contract from a high-tech company. The company liked both my firm's proposal and the other firms', and the presentation before their decision committee, which included their CEO and other C-level executives, was the final event in their decision process. At that time, I was an effective sales-person, but in no way could I claim to be a dazzling presenter. That worried me, but what worried me even more was that I knew my two rivals were accomplished public speakers. The woman sales executive had been a professional actor earlier in her career and the salesperson from my other competitor was serving as the president of a chapter of Toastmasters.

The day after the three of us delivered our presentations, my contact at the company, who was the vice president of sales, first told me what I feared hearing. My rivals were more polished as presenters and had more professional-looking graphics in their slide show (this was before the advent of PowerPoint). But then he went on to say that his decision committee awarded the Ron Volper Group the business. I was stunned, but delighted. The next day we met for lunch, and I was able to debrief him more fully about the presentations. He told me some things at that luncheon that I have never forgotten. Though both of my competitors gave sales presentations that were more dazzling than mine, he said, "Your firm had a better grasp of our needs."

Preparation Was the Key to My Successful Sales Presentation

Here's what I did to prepare for my sales presentation and what my competitors (to my surprise) failed to do. First, I asked my contact if I could call and introduce myself to his colleagues who would be attending the presentation. He agreed to do that, and also agreed to send them a note letting them know I would be calling. Besides that, I asked him to give me the correct spelling and pronunciation of their names. When I got them on the phone, after introducing myself, I:

» Congratulated them on their company's record profits in the last quarter.

» Built rapport with them by listening to and acknowledging their sales challenges.

» Asked them how they perceived the need.

» Asked what they wanted me to focus on during my presentation.

» Identified their decision criteria.

Win the Business *Before* You Show Up for Your Sales Presentation

The goal of a sales presentation is not just to inform or convince, but to create as much momentum in your favor as possible in order to win the business. You can win the business from cautious customers before you show up for your presentation by learning about and controlling both the logistics and the content beforehand. In their rush to make a sale, many new salespeople who are not yet where they want to be in their numbers, weaken their presentation because they don't ask enough questions about the logistics of the presentation and about their customers' expectations regarding the content. To strengthen your presentation and build your confidence, inquire about the following as far in advance of the presentation as possible:

» The time and place of the presentation.

» How much time you have.

» What equipment and materials the customer will make available and what you should bring.

» The names and titles of attendees, and some information about them, including their phone numbers and e-mail (if your contact is willing to provide them).

» What other companies will be presenting and when.

Create a Winning Presentation by First Writing an Agenda

Only after you know the logistics and expectations for your talk can you begin to focus on the content of your presentation. You've probably worked hard to establish credibility so you would be invited to give a presentation. Don't blow it by giving a boilerplate talk or, even worse, "winging it" without any preparation at all. Customers and especially senior-level decision-makers want to know that you've taken the time to learn about their company and the specific ways that your company can help them achieve their goals. This means knowing their company's objectives, needs, and key issues, and understanding their culture. Incorporating their products and terminology into your examples enhances your credibility.

Unless your customer has provided you with an agenda, make a detailed agenda of the structure of your talk *before* writing it. I often use the following eight-point format for my presentations:

1. Introduce myself and my company, and thank them for their time.

2. Give an overview of my agenda and make sure that it meets their expectations.

3. Confirm their objectives and needs, and invite them to expand on them.

4. Present my recommendations and ask for their reactions.

5. Discuss fees and return on investment.

6. Propose next steps.

7. Answer any questions and recap key points.

8. Thank them and my contact, and mention when and how I will follow up.

A "T-3" Overview Provides Structure to Your Presentation

In a sales presentation, where you are attempting to persuade your audience that your proposed solution is best, it is critical that your audience be able to easily follow the entire flow of your presentation, from its beginning to its conclusion. To that end, the "T-3 method" can help your audience see the overall structure of your presentation. T-3 stands for:

» Tell them what you are going to tell them.

» Tell them.

» Tell them what you've told them.

Using PowerPoint and Handouts

Nowadays, many salespeople use PowerPoint in their sales presentations, but many rely on it too much and make some classic mistakes. Use PowerPoint to reinforce your key points, not as a way to introduce them. Your slides are intended to focus your audience's attention and to help them recall the highlights of your presentation, so use it sparingly. Here are some do's and don'ts when using PowerPoint in your sales presentations:

Do use 10 or fewer slides in a 60-minute presentation.

Don't use more than 10 words per slide.

Do use easy-to-read fonts.

Don't use fonts smaller than 30 points.

Do use graphics or bullets for your key points.

Don't read the slides aloud.

Do tell your customers what is *not* on the slides.

Don't depend on your PowerPoint to carry your presentation.

Do practice your sales presentation using your PowerPoint slides.

Handouts with your key points can be effective during a sales presentation so your customers can jot down notes or questions as they follow along. Because handouts represent you and your company, take the time to make them professional-looking. For an added touch, you can add color graphics or include your customer's company name or logo.

However, even when you've completed this critical part of your preparation, you're not finished. Your next step is to practice and polish your sales presentation.

Perfect Practice Makes Perfect Presentations

World renowned pianist Arthur Rubinstein once remarked, "If I skip practice for one day, I know the difference. If I skip practice for two days, my orchestra knows the difference. If I skip practice for three days, my audience knows the difference." However, the comment from the master musician deserves clarification: Practice does not make perfect. As my golf pro keeps telling me, "Perfect practice makes perfect."

Whenever I give a sales presentation, deliver a speech, or conduct a seminar, I practice not only at home or in my office, but at the actual venue the day before or at least before my customers arrive. I want to walk around the room and get a sense of what the environment is like. I pay close attention to the arrangement of the chairs and tables as I practice moving around the room. I pay attention to the acoustics, the lighting, and especially the room temperature. Although I usually project a carefree approach, the truth is, I rehearse everything as much as I can ahead of time.

Arrive Early, Attend to Details, and Greet Your Customers at the Door

I strongly recommend that you show up an hour or so prior to your sales presentation so that you can set up the room, check out the equipment, arrange your materials, and give your introduction a run-through before your company contact or customers arrive. If you have time and you want to get something to drink or eat that's fine, but be ready to devote your entire attention to the attendees the moment they enter the room. One of my most embarrassing experiences as a manager with one of my salespeople was when he arrived late for his own presentation and, before greeting any of the attendees, went straight over to the refreshment table and stuffed a pastry in his mouth. You never want to be seen with food or gum in your mouth when you're about to give a sales presentation.

Small things can make or break your sales presentation. For example, I once attended a presentation where the salesperson was using an LCD projector for his PowerPoint. The presenter neglected to tape the extension cord down, and one of the attendees on the decision committee tripped over the wire. The committee member was not hurt, but he was embarrassed; and it may not have been a coincidence that that salesperson was not awarded the business. A roll of duct tape and attention to this detail might have made the difference between winning and losing a sale.

Greet your customers as they enter the room and introduce yourself if you haven't yet met in person. Smile and make eye contact as you shake hands. Thank them again for taking the time to talk to you during your prior conversation and for attending your presentation. Doing this reminds them that you previously took the time to find out their needs and that your current presentation will address those issues.

It's Not Just What You Say—It's How You Say It

Your delivery is as important as the content of your sales presentation. I urge you not to read your sales presentation. Instead, know what you want to say and have your key points on index cards or on PowerPoint slides. Although you don't have to memorize your entire sale presentation, I do suggest that you memorize the beginning few minutes and the conclusion, including your call to action. This will boost your confidence, make you appear as a more polished speaker, and get the desired results: your customer's agreement to follow your recommendations.

Your Voice, Body Language, and Movements Indicate Your Level of Confidence

Many salespeople talk too fast during their presentations, so don't be afraid to slow down a little. When you speak at a comfortable rate, your audience will see you as more of an authority. If you think you are speaking too slowly, you're probably speaking at just the right speed for your audience. Also, include multiple pauses throughout your presentation, so your customers have time to digest what you've said, and be sure to speak loudly enough or use a microphone so that everyone in the room can hear you.

Vocal quality consists of more than volume and pace. It also includes enunciation—how clearly you articulate the words in your talk, and inflection—how you vary the pitch of your voice. In general, if you can lower your pitch, you'll sound more authoritative and your voice will be more pleasing. Although you should mostly speak in a lower tone, varying your pitch will hold the audience's attention.

Move away from the podium and walk around the room, but do not walk so far into the room that people in the first few rows are looking at your back. Remove anything from your pockets that might distract you or the attendees. This includes electronic devices, such as BlackBerrys, and anything that may jangle, such as keys. Keep your hands hanging at your side, or use them to accentuate key points. Don't fold your arms or hold one hand with the other. It is important to smile at various points throughout your sales presentation, especially at the beginning, when members of the audience bring up a point or ask questions, and, finally, at the end with your conclusion and call to action.

Maintain Good Eye Contact

In a sales presentation (where you'll usually be addressing a small group), you should be able to look at everyone in the audience. The trick is to avoid the windshield wiper effect. That occurs when the speaker abruptly shifts her gaze from one person to another. So try to hold eye contact for approximately three seconds per person. In a sales presentation, you should especially make eye contact with two people in the room: the most senior decision-maker and your contact (especially if your contact is your "sponsor" in the sale. She will often tell you via her body language how you're doing and whether or not you need to modify your style during the presentation).

Interact With Attendees

Our customer surveys show that the most successful salespeople interact a great deal with the customers in the audience by asking questions and encouraging them to share their insights and suggestions. One way to do this is to stop after each part of your presentation and ask if they have any questions, or would like to comment on or add anything to what you've said. Another way to encourage their participation is to ask them questions about their objectives and needs, and the progress they have made in attacking the issue thus far. As much as possible, also refer to your prior conversation with individuals in the audience.

Keep Them Engaged and Interested With Humor, Anecdotes, and Data

You can make your sales presentation more interesting by weaving in relevant anecdotes, case studies, and personal stories from your professional experience. If you are able to inject humor into it, you make your presentation that much more enjoyable for attendees. Be sure that your humor is appropriate, however. Avoid mentioning anything that might make anyone in the room or with their company or yours uncomfortable. In general, gently poking fun at yourself or telling a G-rated anecdote to prove a point works well.

For example, I recently received an effusive introduction from a customer before my talk. I thanked him for his kind words and said, "Bill, thank you for reading that introduction just the way my mother wrote it." I also got a laugh from attendees when I said at a talk I gave to an industry association, "Please feel free to interrupt me at any time...with applause." Then I quickly added, "Questions are okay, too."

At a time when most customers are skeptical about what they hear and cautious about making decisions, you must work extra hard to convince those attending the sales presentation that your recommendations or company's products will help achieve their desired results. To mitigate customer doubt and build your credibility, cite published data from third parties and customer testimonials as successful examples of how your company has helped your customers achieve their business goals.

Responding to Questions

In a sales presentation the way you respond to questions can determine whether or not you win the business. You improve your chances by doing the following:

» Anticipate questions in advance by asking your contact what issues or questions are likely to be raised.

» Jot down the essentials of any questions the audience asks you.

» Paraphrase the gist of the question in your own words.

» Try to respond briefly but specifically.

» Check back with questioners to ensure you answered the question to their satisfaction.

If you don't know the answer to a question, say so. But tell questioners you will look into it and get back to them, and then be sure to follow up.

After the Presentation

At the conclusion of your presentation, it's sometimes a nice touch to give each attendee a token gift, especially if you can connect the gift thematically with something their company or your company does. Coffee mugs and t-shirts are fallback items. You enhance their perceived value if you personalize a gift with each attendee's name. Check with your contact to be sure that even an inexpensive item does not violate their company's policy. Be sure to follow-up with your contact and attendees after the presentation. Although e-mail arrives instantly, a personal handwritten note on a greeting card thanking them for the opportunity to speak to their group has more impact.

A Final Few Words About Your Sales Presentations

Delivering an effective sales presentation takes lots of work, but giving it prematurely can ruin a sale, so take the time needed to prepare and practice. Be sure you can answer key questions about the company's objectives, needs, and current situation, and know who will be involved in the decision and what their decision criteria are before you speak. Finally, think of sales presentations as sales calls on many customers simultaneously. Your goal is to gain and keep their attention so you can convince them that you fully understand what it is they are trying to achieve, and then offer the best recommendations to enable them to realize their goals.

Strategy 8

Deliver Proposals to Hard-to-Please Customers

> *The Executive Summary is the most read part of a sales proposal and, along with the Investment Schedule, is the part that most influences customers in their decision process.*
> —Ron Volper Group 2010 Sales Study

As mentioned, after completing two stellar years in sales, and being named Salesperson of the Year, at the beginning of my third year, I fell into a slump, and was desperate to make a sale. Early one Monday morning the phone rang in my office. It was the vice president of sales with a Fortune 500 company, located less than a mile from my office. He said that his company was about to award a major contract for sales consulting and sales training services to a consulting firm by the end of the week, and at the last minute one of his sales managers mentioned that my firm had expertise in those areas and should be added to the list of potential vendors for the project.

I said I was interested in learning more and suggested we meet later that day or the next day. The VP said he was heading out of town for several days and neither he nor anyone else at his company was available to meet with me. Instead, he offered to fill me in during that phone call, so that I could submit a detailed sales proposal. When I asked if we could meet to discuss my sales proposal, he said he wanted me to send it to him, so he could review it first. I reluctantly agreed to his request, and spent two days crafting a sales proposal based on the information he had given me.

I dropped off our proposal several days later, but neither the VP nor anyone else in his company was available to meet with me at the time. And to my chagrin, despite my many phone calls, letters, faxes and even a visit, I never heard from him—or anyone else at his company— again. Though that happened some 30 years ago, it was one of the most painful but instructive lessons in my sales career.

Why You Write a Sales Proposal

A sales proposal should not contain any surprises to the customer. It is intended to confirm what you and the customer have essentially agreed to, flesh out the details, and do the following:

1. Reiterate your understanding of the customers' needs and business objectives.

2. Present your recommendations and the benefits flowing from them.

3. Explain your firm's added value and justify the customers' return on investment.

4. Enhance your credibility with the customer and differentiate your company from the competition.

When (and When Not) to Write a Sales Proposal

Here's what I learned from that experience: If the customer is too busy to meet with you (both to share her needs and then to discuss your sales proposal), you're too busy to waste time writing it. Yet, I see many salespeople, especially those who are behind in their numbers, writing sales proposals prematurely— or even worse, writing proposals that are unqualified. The fact is that wherever you are against your sales goals, you don't have time to waste going down a blind alley.

A sales proposal is like a sales presentation, in that you win the business before writing it—or you don't. In fact, the salespeople who win the most business are the ones who meet with customers earliest in the sales cycle and are able to help customers develop the specifications for the Request for Proposal, so that they can shape the RFP to highlight their company's strengths.

What You Need to Know Before Agreeing to Write a Sales Proposal

To save you time and trouble, find out the following about the sales opportunity before agreeing to write a proposal:

- » Your customer's needs and business objectives as they relate to your product or service.
- » Their budget.
- » Which other companies are competing for this business (and ideally why they were invited to compete).
- » Their decision criteria.
- » Who will be involved in making the decision and what the steps in the decision process are for the given company.
- » When they will be making the decision.
- » How they will measure the effectiveness of your product or service.

And, as it relates to the actual sales proposal, you also need to know:

- » What information the company wants included in the sales proposal.
- » If the company has developed a formal Request for Proposal or has a preferred proposal format.

9 Parts of a Sales Proposal

If my customer does not have a sales proposal format, depending upon my discussion with him, I usually include the following sections in my sales proposals:

1. Cover Page

The cover page creates the first impression, so be sure it conveys the following information, and does so in a professional and attractive manner:

» **Sales Proposal Title.** An effective sales proposal title conveys the benefit of what you're proposing. For example, when my firm recently presented a sales proposal for a sales consulting project, the title was "A Sales Proposal to Conduct a Sales Analysis to Accelerate Revenues for ABC Company."

» **Proposal Date.** This is the date you will be presenting it to the client (not the date you wrote it). Your proposal's date establishes the "start time" for your client to review and respond to recommendations.

» **Client Company and Optionally Each Recipient's Name.** Check and double-check the spelling of the client's name and job title, company name, and address.

» **Your Company's Name and your Contact Information.** If appropriate, include an alternate person to contact if you are not available.

If your sales proposal contains proprietary or confidential information, you can include the following statement on the cover page: "The information in this proposal is confidential and proprietary and may not be shared in any form or format with anyone outside [the customer's company] without the written permission of [insert your company's name]."

Q: What is the most common mistake on a sales proposal's cover page?

A: Typos and misspelling the client's name.

2. Table of Contents

The table of contents lists in order each section of your sales proposal, including page numbers. While some clients will read your proposal from beginning to end, others will first turn to the sections that interest them the most, such as the Executive Summary and the Investment Schedule.

Q: What is the most common mistake in a table of contents?

A: Incorrect page numbers.

3. Executive Summary

An Executive Summary is an overview of your proposal, including the client's needs, options, benefits of your recommendations, and results your customer can anticipate. Fees and price are not included in the Executive Summary. According to the Ron Volper Group 2010 Sales Study, many C-level executives read the Executive Summary before anything else.

The Executive Summary also allows you to highlight your firm's strengths, describe how you are different from your competition, offer greater added-value, and convey a theme about your company that you can reiterate throughout the document.

Q: What are the most common mistakes in the Executive Summary of a sales proposal?

A: They are too long and include too much vendor boasting.

4. Customer's Needs and Objectives as They Relate to the Project

This section of the sales proposal defines the client's specific problems, opportunities, and/or objectives that the recommendations in your sales proposal promise to address. It is critical to match the scope of your work articulated in your proposal with those needs, opportunities, and objectives defined by the client.

Q: What are the most common mistakes in a sales proposal's client needs assessment?

A: Not specific enough to accurately define the scope of work.

5. Company Status, Business Focus, and Past Efforts Related to Your Sales Proposal's Objectives

This section briefly describes the company's current market position, focus, and goals. Include in this section key actions they've taken that are related to the defined objectives in your sales proposal. Did their actions get the desired results and, if so, to what degree? The purpose of this section is to create continuity with earlier efforts and the recommendations listed in your sales proposal, so it is important to be as positive as you can about the company's past initiatives and results.

Q: What are the most common mistakes in a sales proposal's company status section?

A: Harsh criticism, blatant flattery of past efforts, or overly general statements.

6. Recommendations and Benefits

Your sales proposal's recommendations are a description of the scope of work you or your company intend to perform to address your client's defined needs, opportunities, and/or objectives. The benefits you promise are the results, or outcomes, that the company will reap if they accept your proposal and follow your recommendations.

Q: What are the most common mistakes in a sales proposal's recommendations and benefits?

A: Recommendations that are vague, are non-specific, and over-promise benefits.

7. Investment Schedule

The investment schedule in your sales proposal delineates your fees for each part of the project or for each product or service that you will deliver. It also includes your payment terms and any other clarifying information, such as additional costs, and how the project can be modified or cancelled.

*Q: **What are the most common mistakes in a sales proposal's Investment Schedule?***

*A: **Underestimating or omitting costs and omitting a return on investment analysis.***

8. Time Frame

This section of your proposal breaks down all the key events, or deliverables, into a time line so that your client knows what to expect from you and when you will deliver it. In addition, the time frame includes what you expect and require the customer to do to facilitate the project.

*Q: **What are the most common mistakes in a sales proposal's time frame?***

*A: **Not factoring in unexpected delays either by the client, vendor, weather, availability of needed materials, or other factors that can affect a project's completion, and not listing your expectations as to what the client needs to provide and when.***

9. Appendices

The appendices in your proposal serve a variety of functions, including:

» Describing any of the other sections in greater detail.

» Elaborating on what you have learned about the issue.

» Offering more detailed discussion of the project's projected return on investment.

» Bios of your project leaders and team.

» Information about your company, including sample clients.

» References.

More Ways to Enhance the Readability of Your Sales Proposal

The proposal reflects who you are and what your company stands for, so make it attractive and professional-looking. Though many companies request electronic copies of sales proposals, a hard copy can be more impactful. The best sales proposals are neat, concise, applicable to the client's needs, and easy to read. Here are more ways to make your proposals stand out and be accepted:

» Increase the readability of your sales proposal by using short sentences, bullets, and common words.

» Customize your sales proposal with your company logo.

» Use the customer's technical terms—not your company jargon—to demonstrate that you understand their business and corporate culture.

» Keep the formatting simple by using easy-to-read 12-point fonts, such as Times New Roman, Arial, or Courier.

» Use 1-inch margins and, if applicable, double space.

» Print in color when appropriate.

» Use boldface, italics, and other fonts sparingly.

» If appropriate, use charts and graphs to illustrate data.

» Proofread, or have a colleague proofread, your sales proposal at least twice.

» Print your sales proposal on high-quality paper with a fresh ink cartridge.

» Bind your proposal with spiral binding or velo binding. Include a clear plastic cover and cardstock back.

Differentiating Your Company in the Sales Proposal

One of the ways I have differentiated my firm and won business is by including a link in my sales proposal to a video. For example, in a recent sales proposal to design compensation plans for a global beverage company, I included a link to a video I created about my firm's philosophy on how to compensate salespeople and others. Another way to differentiate your company is simply to include photos of each team member next to their biographies.

13 Things to Do to Present Your Sales Proposal to Cautious Customers

One of the biggest mistakes salespeople make is sending the proposal rather than presenting it in person. Another mistake they make is handing it to the customer rather than walking them through it and using it to stimulate further discussion. Here are more ways to shorten the sales cycle and increase your chances of getting your proposal accepted:

1. Before officially submitting your sales proposal, if possible, informally preview it with your customer to insure that he or she is comfortable with what you've proposed.

2. Request that all the decision-makers attend the meeting when you do formally present your proposal.

3. Although you will lead this meeting, encourage your customers to participate in the discussion.

4. Reiterate the background for and objectives of the proposal.

5. Tell attendees that your proposal is intended as "a stake in the ground" to spur further thought and discussion, and, as such, is subject to revision based on their input.

6. Say, "With your permission, I would like to use the following process to review my proposal. I have highlighted key sections and would like you to then read those sections, ask questions, and share your thoughts."

7. Continue to summarize their needs and offer your recommendations.

8. Distribute the sales proposal and ask them to read the Executive Summary. Ask if they have any questions or have any corrections to offer.

9. Review and ask them to read the section on objectives. Ask if there are any questions or comments. To facilitate interaction, leave several blank bullets in various parts of the proposal, so attendees can add their ideas to what you have written. They'll feel more involved and you'll get better buy-in from them.

10. Move to the section on your recommendations. First, summarize your recommendations. Next ask them to read that part of your proposal, and then ask for their reaction.

11. Comment on the process you will use to implement the program or product, directing their attention to the appropriate pages.

12. Summarize the section on fees, have them read the appropriate pages, and ask for and answer any questions. Reiterate the value they will receive and the return on investment they can anticipate.

13. Before concluding the meeting, ask if there are any other questions. Then ask for their overall reaction to your sales proposal.

A Polished Sales Proposal Is the Step that Leads to Sealing the Deal

You've done your homework and determined that the time was right to write a proposal. You made sure to include the nine essentials parts that make up a successful sales proposal—and double-checked it for accuracy, neatness, and clarity. You even practiced answering the objections you expect your customer to bring up during your face-to-face presentation.

If their response to your proposal is positive, recommend a next step, or ask them what has to happen next to consummate the deal. When you return to your office, send them a follow-up note thanking them for their time, reiterating what you and they have agreed to, reinforcing the idea that you would like to do business with them, and letting them know you are confident that you will meet and exceed their expectations for the project.

Strategy 9

Enlist Customers to Help You Develop New Business

If you call prospects cold there is only a 2 percent chance you will speak to them, if you have a referral your odds jump to 20 percent, but if you have an introduction they jump up to 60 percent.
—Ron Volper Group 2010 Sales Study

When I ran sales for a Fortune 500 Company, Amy was one of my most talented sales executives. Of the many salespeople I managed, she had the best close rate of anyone on my team. Her skill at closing business enabled her to be my top producer in only her second year with the company. But paradoxically, it also caused her near downfall! Because she had such a high conversion rate, she spent less time than her peers in prospecting for new business, and most months she had the lowest number of prospects in her pipeline.

In the first quarter of her third year, she had a rude awakening. Virtually all of her accounts, including the ones that she forecast as having a high probability of closing, fell out of her pipeline, and she was only able to close one small piece of business for the entire quarter. This caused her to go from first to worst in her numbers, and during the following quarter, she fell into a slump.

To her credit, she recognized that her problem was not her sales skills, but that she had been overconfident and over-reliant on too few accounts. After that jolt of reality, she worked

95

diligently at filling her pipeline with prospects, and by the last quarter, she was way over plan and back among my top producers.

One of the reasons salespeople get into a slump is that they spend too little time prospecting for new business. A related reason is that they don't have a new business development plan.

New business can be developed from the following six sources:

1. Referrals from customers.

2. Referrals from non-customers.

3. Planned networking.

4. Unplanned networking.

5. Referrals from third parties.

6. Prospecting by mail, e-mail, and phone.

Referrals From Customers

One of the best ways for salespeople in a slump to get back on track (besides cross-selling products to existing customers) is to ask for referrals from existing customers. Yet, the salespeople who need business the most—the ones in a slump—often do it least, whereas the salespeople who need it least—the ones already exceeding their goals—ask for it most.

To obtain referrals from existing customers, make sure you have met their expectations and let them know that you appreciate their business. The best way to show customers you appreciate their business is by doing a good job on the delivery of the product or service you promised. The second way is by continuously communicating with customers so they are fully aware of what you're doing and why at each stage of the project. The third way to show you appreciate customers' business is by doing something "special" for them. This can consist of:

» Referring business to them.

» Taking them to a ballgame or the theater.

» Inviting them to a company event, such as a golf outing or picnic.

» Giving them some information that would be useful for them.

» Sending them a book or article.

» Sending them a birthday card.

» Congratulating them on some personal or business achievement.

When and How Do You Ask Customers for a Referral?

Generally speaking, if you're not sure when to ask a customer for a referral, the answer is "right now." More specifically, ask customers whenever they signal they are pleased with something you've done for them. Besides reluctance to being turned down, one of the reasons salespeople are sometimes uncomfortable asking for a referral is that they don't know what to say. Here's what I've found works best for me. Feel free to adapt it so that it works for you:

"John, I've greatly enjoyed our relationship and working with you and your colleagues. As is true for your company's salespeople, my business has grown because of referrals from good people like yourself. Can you suggest one or two CEOs or heads of sales you know who are also looking to accelerate sales that my company might be able to help?"

If your customer is kind enough to give you a name and phone number, thank him, but don't stop there. Cold calling gives you only a 2-percent chance of getting through to a prospect. Having a referral increases your chances to 20 percent, but obtaining an introduction ups your chances of getting through to 60 percent. So, after getting a name, ask your customer if he would mind introducing you.

Referrals From Non-Customers

Years ago, I stumbled upon another way to generate referrals. I had cold-called the head of sales at a major hotel company. We built good rapport and had a good conversation, but he turned me down on the next step, as he had recently retained one of my competitors to conduct a sales consulting project. As I started to walk out of his office, he called me back, wrote down the name and phone number of another head of sales at a hotel company that served a different market segment than his company, and said I should give her a call and use his name. I did so, and to my surprise, his lead led me to a sizable piece of business and a 10-year business relationship with that hotel company. After that, I began to ask even people who turned me down if they could suggest anyone else I should contact. Most said "no," but several gave me contacts that led to business.

Planned and Impromptu Networking

Top salespeople attend more networking events and network more effectively than their peers. It's unfortunate that more salespeople don't use networking because it is one of the best ways to prevent yourself from falling into a slump and getting out of one if you do. There are two types of networking: planned and impromptu.

Planned networking consists of attending scheduled meetings or events, whereas impromptu networking consists of meeting people by chance. There are three types of networking groups you can join:

1. Business groups that are exclusively or primarily devoted to fostering networking, so members can expand their business.

2. Business groups not exclusively devoted to networking, but that have networking as part of their mission.

3. Organizations that are not business-related, but can nevertheless help you gain referrals and grow your business.

Develop a Networking Strategy

Top salespeople attend networking events three times more often than their peers. But besides showing up more often, they have a networking strategy and use a networking plan. They scan the business media for networking events and put these meetings on their calendar weeks and even months ahead of time. They'll often attend two or three networking events in a week, whereas salespeople in a slump typically attend none.

They join local business groups devoted to networking and conscientiously attend their meetings. But as mentioned, they also join other organizations (cultural, civic, fraternal, philanthropic, religious, and educational) that are not formally devoted to networking, but where they can meet people.
For example, some of the best business contacts I've made came through the Newcomer's Club when my wife and I moved into our new home in New York State.

One of the ways I decided which groups to join was to ask my clients which organizations they belonged to. Because my best clients are CEOs of companies, soon after establishing my firm, I joined the Young President's Club and the CEO Club. Because I enjoy bike riding, I joined a local bike club. Because I do a great deal of public speaking, I joined a chapter of Toastmasters International and the National Speakers Association.

Besides planning which groups to affiliate with, top salespeople also plan which people they would like to meet at an event. Many organizations make the list of attendees available prior to the event, and others have a list of attendees at the event. In either case, it's worthwhile to scan it and decide whom you would like to talk to before you step into the meeting room. If you get there early and the list of attendees is not available, you can scan the name tags that are usually arranged alphabetically on the reception table to see who will be attending the event.

What to Do and Not Do at a Networking Event

It's important to join the right groups, but it's equally important to do the right things when you attend their events. One of the ways I sometimes motivate myself to meet as many people as feasible at a networking group is to create a friendly competition with a colleague to see which one of us can gather more business cards. If I'm there by myself, I give myself a goal in which I try to gain more referrals than on a previous occasion. The caveat to this is that the name of the game is establishing relationships, not collecting business cards.

Although it's important to solidify relationships with people you already know, your primary goal in attending a networking event is to meet new people. So avoid spending too much time with those you already know and instead devote most of your time to getting to know new people.

I find the easiest way to meet new people is look at someone who is not talking to someone else, smile at him, walk over with my hand outstretched, and introduce myself. I then ask him questions regarding the following:

- » How he is enjoying the event.
- » If he is a member of the organization.
- » What he does for a living and how he got into the business.
- » Which other organizations he belongs to and why.
- » Who he is looking to meet.

You could also compliment the person on something he or she is wearing, such as a tie for a man or a pin for a woman. Remember: What's more important than what you say is that you come across as upbeat and enthusiastic.

If you can say something humorous about the event or anything else, assuming it is in totally good taste, you'll build relationships even sooner. Before discussing business with someone, try to find a shared connection: favorite teams, hobbies, where she lives, grew up, or attended college, and so forth. A networking conversation is a bit like a sales call in that your goal is to get the other person talking—especially about himself or herself—before you start talking about yourself. One of the best things you can say is: "I'd like to be helpful to you; who are you looking to meet at this event and more generally?"

Practice your 30-second "elevator talk" until you can comfortably communicate the benefits of what you do (that is, what problems you help people solve or what opportunities you help them take advantage of). For example, as a sales consultant, when asked that question, I often say: "I help companies increase sales and improve sales force efficiency by providing their executives and salespeople with information, ideas, tools, and training."

Even if you think someone at the event is a good prospect for your business, do not attempt to sell him on anything. Instead, after talking with him, suggest that the two of you get together at a later time, and exchange business cards. Men should keep their cards in their jacket pocket, and women in a similarly accessible place. Some salespeople jot down a few key words on the person's business card to remind them about the person when they return to their office. This is a worthwhile practice. Try to limit your conversation with each person to about five to seven minutes so you can meet as many people as possible.

If the conversation has gone well, and you've offered to help him meet others, ask him if there is anyone else in the room that he can introduce you to.

How to Comfortably Conclude the Conversation

Many people find it awkward to break off the conversation with someone they've just met. I've seen people at networking events offend the person they just had a good conversation with by abruptly saying "excuse me" and then walking away.

In my experience a better way is to say something such as the following: "I've enjoyed talking with you, Joe, but I'm sure you want to meet other people too, so let me not monopolize your time. I'll call you within a few days to see if we can continue our conversation over a cup of coffee and see how we can help each other."

Unplanned Networking

The networking I just described constitutes pre-planned networking, but impromptu networking can be just as valuable. One salesperson I managed worked himself out of a slump and became salesperson of the year by adopting what I call the 3-foot rule. If the circumstances permitted it, he would strike up a conversation with any respectable-looking person within 3 feet. He struck up conversations with people on airplanes, trains, and even elevators. He told all of his friends, neighbors, relatives, and people he bought from what he did for a living and asked them for referrals. And he got—and gave—quite a few.

My own experience with impromptu networking is perhaps even more telling. The year after I started my firm, I had a very small pipeline and a large amount of trepidation about where my next client would come from. That summer, my wife and I rented a beach house for our vacation. I was standing by the water's edge one morning, watching my two young kids make sand pies, when I noticed there was another man standing right near me who was watching his young son playing in the water. I struck up a conversation with him and learned that he was the founder and CEO of a well-known investment banking firm that held financial positions in more than 50 different companies. Soon after I returned from my vacation, I called the CEO and arranged to meet with him in his office. He introduced me to the president of a major paper company that they had just taken a stake in. That introduction culminated in a major project for my firm, and I went on to establish a long-standing relationship with the CEO, during which time we worked with 12 different companies in his investment firm's portfolio. All this came about because I practiced the 3-foot rule.

Referrals From Third Parties

In thinking about organizations you should join and events you should attend, keep in mind that you can often develop relationships with third parties (also known as intermediaries) who can refer you to customers, even though they themselves may never use your product or services. For example, bankers can recommend attorneys and accountants and vice versa; financial planners can recommend insurance brokers, accountants, and attorneys; and real estate brokers can recommend professionals who do carpentry, plumbing, electricity, and mortgages, insurance.

Besides belonging to more organizations than their peers, top salespeople are more active in the organizations they affiliate themselves with. By serving as president of a chapter of the National Speaker's Association, as a board member of the Hospitality Sales and Marketing Association, and on the nominating committee for the Board of the Westchester County Association, I have increased my visibility, met some great people, and gotten (and given) referrals that led to several pieces of business.

Prospecting by Mail

Although gaining referrals from customers or through networking is the best way to break out of a slump or reach the next level in sales, in most cases, that by itself won't fill your new business pipeline, so you'll also have to generate leads by contacting prospects cold. You'll be able to get through to only a very small percent, and an even smaller percent will be willing to meet with you, but you should keep at it nevertheless. One of the ways to increase your chances of getting through is by first sending a letter and then calling. Though e-mail is quicker, easier, and less expensive than regular mail, because fewer people now use it, regular mail stands out and is now more likely to be read—especially if you customize your letter to recipients and demonstrate that you know something about their company.

If your budget allows, send the letter via UPS, FedEx, or Airborne, as it is more likely to be noticed and read. Second- or third-day delivery is cheaper and works just as well as over-night delivery. I recommend you send out as many letters as you can realistically follow up on during the next week and no more. If you send out your letters on a Thursday or Friday, they will likely reach your prospect the middle of the following week, which is often the best time to make a follow-up phone call.

Prospecting by Phone

Whether you've gotten their name from a referral or gen-erated your own lead, one of the important steps to developing new business is calling people on the phone to set a time for a face-to-face meeting. I recommend you make as many calls as possible before 8 a.m., after 5:30 p.m., or during lunchtime, when the gatekeeper is less likely to be present. Though you may have to deal with voice mail, you've eliminated the human screen, and if the executive is in her office, she may very well pick up the phone herself. Because you won't be able to make all your calls when the gatekeeper is away, if you're calling a senior executive, you'll likely reach the gatekeeper on occa-sion. The trick here is not to try to blow by gatekeepers but to enlist their help. This means explaining what you're trying to do and asking them for their suggestion as to how you can get through to the person you're trying to reach. Before you do so, give them a short and sweet reason why their boss would benefit by speaking with you.

Because these days most customers are time-deprived, you'll need to capture the decision-maker's attention on the phone in 20 seconds or less. Although the reality is that many prospects will not take your call, or be willing to see you, I find the following approach often works for me in getting them to agree to a meeting (of course, I modify my approach based on who I am calling and how they respond):

"Good morning, Mr. Jones. This is Ron Volper, managing partner of the Ron Volper Group, following up on the letter I recently sent you. Do you have a moment to talk? We're a 25 year-old management consulting firm that has helped 87 Fortune 500 Companies and 300 other major companies measurably increase sales. Your company has been successful, but may I ask you how satisfied you are with your current level of sales?

"Based on our experience with other companies in your industry and my research I have several ideas that might help your company build on its success. I'd like to spend 30 minutes with you to brief you on what we've learned about how successful companies like yours can increase sales (reduce their cost-of-sales), and see whether or not we can help you accelerate your growth. Which days next week or the following are you available for a cup of coffee?"

In a Down Market, It's More Important Than Ever to Network

Notice in the previous example I elected not to ask whether the executive received my letter. This is because there is a good chance he won't remember it, and he might ask me to resend it. However, if I did ask if he received it and he said, "No. Could you resend it?" rather than doing so (and lengthening the sales cycle), I would say: "Let me tell you what it said," and summarize it in a single sentence. Whether you do it through (planned or impromptu) networking or cold calling, continually filling your pipeline and focusing on new business development is one of the best ways to get out of a slump—and prevent yourself from falling into one in the first place.

Practice Sales Habits That Appeal to Cautious Customers

Salespeople who describe themselves as having a more positive attitude make 20 percent more face-to-face calls and more often than their peers attain their revenue goals.
—Ron Volper Group 2010 Sales Study

At the age of 39, Franklin D. Roosevelt contracted polio, yet his can-do attitude enabled him to deal with this crippling disease, become the longest-serving president of the United States, and steer the country through the Great Depression and most of World War II. FDR's accomplishments can be traced in part to his embodying the belief that a positive attitude can overcome adversity. The same principle can apply to salespeople struggling to meet their sales goals.

A Negative Attitude Will Sink Your Sales

It's natural for a salesperson's attitude to sink if his or her sales fail to meet projected goals. When sales sag, even hard-working reps tend to get down on themselves and lose confidence in their company's products or services. If left unchecked, their "stinkin' thinkin'" causes a decrease in the quantity and quality of sales activities, which, in turn, negatively affects their sales results. Salespeople whose sales are down or whose companies are falling short of their revenue or profit goals need to regain a positive sales attitude about their own abilities before they can expect to have the right attitude toward their customers.

One sign of a falling sales attitude is an increase in *call reluctance*. Pessimistic salespeople who are struggling tend to make fewer phone calls to get appointments and make fewer face-to-face sales calls. In addition, while on sales calls, salespeople who are behind in their numbers ask 40 percent fewer questions than their peers. As a result, they achieve their stated call objectives 30 percent less often than their high-performing peers. Moreover, their negative self-talk often intrudes upon their ability to listen, and they often miss crucial information from customers.

12 Ways to Help Raise a Sagging Sales Attitude

If you are falling short of your sales goals, you may feel down. The following tips and strategies can help you lift a sagging sales attitude.

1. Make More Calls and Better Sales Calls

Our survey of sales activities suggests that when top salespeople are not happy with their sales figures, they don't give up, blame the economy, or blame their competition. Like the struggling professional baseball player in a hitting slump, they go "back to basics" and double-up on their efforts to break out of the doldrums. They make sure—no matter how they feel—that they meet or exceed the number of customer calls, and the calls move the sale forward. The point here is: Don't count the sales; count the calls—and sooner than you might expect, your sales attitude (and actual sales) will improve.

2. Use Meditation to Relax

Meditation is a great way to help you calm down and build positive feelings about yourself. According to our findings, salespeople who engage in meditation experience less emotional turmoil—and bounce back more quickly when they are down in the dumps. The most successful salesperson I ever managed (the one who consistently earned the most and was most respected by our customers), meditated every morning for 30 minutes. With a clear mind, it's not surprising that he had an upbeat attitude and was a great listener who easily built rapport with customers. However, there are several scientific studies that suggest that even if you meditate for just 10 minutes every other day, you will feel better and do better.

Although there are many books and programs on how to meditate, the essence of meditation is to sit quietly, either in a cross-legged position or on a comfortable chair, with erect posture, and concentrate on your breath as you inhale and exhale. Some people who meditate make their exhaled breath approximately twice as long as their inhaled breath, but that is not essential. If your mind wanders, gently bring your thoughts back to your breathing. Some people find it helpful to think of a trigger word, such as the word *relax* or the word *calm,* to help them relax during their meditation.

3. Visualize Desired Outcomes

Visualization is another way that salespeople can boost their sales attitude. This means sitting quietly and creating a positive mental picture of a desired outcome with plenty of details. For example, I like to visualize myself entering a prospect's office, and engaging him or her in a friendly "sales" conversation that puts a smile on both of our faces. Visualization is a relaxation technique that can easily be combined with meditation.

4. Use Yoga to Relax Your Body and Mind

As is the case with many other successful salespeople I know, yoga exercises are my favorite way to relax my muscles, reduce stress, and put myself in the right frame of mind to make lots of sales calls. Yoga's popularity continues to grow because there are many opportunities to incorporate the exercises into your daily sales routine. You can do yoga on your own with or without a television program or an audio or video program, or you can join yoga classes offered in your community.

5. Participate in Fun Physical Activities

A sales executive for a major insurance company I was coaching was well below her sales goals going into the third quarter of the year. She was angry and frustrated, and often berated herself. I suggested that, among other things, she needed an outlet to work off her frustrations. Because a friend of hers was a biking enthusiast, she decided to buy a bike and join a bike club. She went from being a sedentary individual to one who biked 100 miles a week. More impressively, she went from 70 percent of her sales goal to 120 percent of her goal and qualified for her company's President's Club (their annual recognition trip to a five-star resort for their sales stars). In fact, she used part of her extra incentive compensation to purchase a new racing bike. Although her newfound interest in biking was not the only reason for her remarkable turnaround, it helped her to relax, improve her attitude, and increase her sales.

If you don't have a favorite physical activity, consider taking up biking, jogging, swimming, hiking, tennis, soccer, or any another sport or activity. It's been scientifically proven that vigorous exercise for 30 minutes or longer causes the body to release a chemical substance called dopamine, which helps people feel better.

6. Spend Time With Optimistic Colleagues

In the same way that your positive sales attitude builds rapport with your customers, you can guard against "creeping pessimism" by avoiding negative people and instead surrounding yourself with colleagues who are actively pursuing their sales and professional goals. Because most of us have relationships with both optimists and pessimists (you can pick your friends, but not your family), make a conscious effort to spend as much time as possible with those people you know with an optimistic approach to achieving their goals.

7. Listen to and Watch Motivational Programs and Read Inspiring Stories

The top-performing salespeople we surveyed also spent more time listening to inspirational or motivational talks and reading inspirational books than their lower-performing colleagues. They are the ones who feed their mind "good stuff" while driving to a call. For example, a number of salespeople we talked to enjoyed reading inspirational books by Dale Carnegie, Napoleon Hill, Norman Vincent Peale, M. Scott Peck, and Eckhart Tolle.

8. Take Small Pleasurable Breaks and a Vacation

Salespeople can also reduce their stress and put themselves in a more positive mood by taking short breaks during the working day. Some successful salespeople give themselves breaks to reward themselves for certain necessary activities. For example, one salesperson I know treats herself to a cappuccino after she completes 10 calls to prospects. Another one goes out for a yogurt after completing a customer proposal. As one top producer put it, "I always remember to play at work and work at play." Although salespeople who are among the top 10 percent work more hours than their peers when they are on the job, they also take more vacations.

9. Help Others to Succeed

After several years as her company's top salesperson, a young woman I know fell into a serious funk and sales slump. Neither she nor her manager could pinpoint the reason for her poor performance, and nothing she did seemed to help improve her negative attitude. One day, she got a call from a volunteer asking her to contribute to the United Way campaign in her town. For some reason, the call resonated with her, so she decided to join the board of the local chapter of United Way and help raise funds. As a result of her calling potential donors and companies to ask for contributions, two things happened. First, she came out of her funk and became the top volunteer fundraiser for United Way in her community. Second, she claims that because her general outlook had improved, she made a large sale for her company to another United Way volunteer who also happened to be the CEO of a successful privately held company.

10. Keep a Success Journal

For struggling salespeople behind in their numbers, a sagging sales attitude can seem overwhelming. One way to help mitigate the impact of a negative outlook is by taking a few minutes each day to write down what you are doing right, proud of, or grateful for in a "Success Journal." Include all daily achievements, even if they're not monumental or not work-related. You'll discover that, even if you are currently disappointed with your sales numbers, you will soon feel a bounce in your attitude and a more optimistic approach to meeting your sales goals.

11. Box in Your Worries

When I asked an elderly friend his secret to his nearly 70-year-long sales career, he replied, "I didn't bring my problems at home to work and I didn't take my problems at work back home." Although everyone has things to worry about at work and home, several top salespeople I've worked with extend my friend's strategy to another method to box in their worries. They will designate a specific time each day as *worry time*. During that brief period of about five minutes, they allow themselves to think about everything they fear might happen on and off the job. But if they start worrying at another time, they stop themselves by saying "It's not yet worry time!"

12. Use Positive Self-Talk

Another way to boost a sagging sales attitude is to use positive self-talk to cancel out any negative internal monologue that diminishes your confidence and motivation. For example, if you lose a sale to a competitor, you might say the following to yourself: "The bad news is that I lost that sale, but I know I am a good salesperson, selling a good product, and I have lots of opportunity to succeed. Learn from the experience and move on. Next time I'll do better."

The Power and Benefit of Daily Attitude-Boosting Activities

Meditating, doing yoga or visualization exercises, reading or listening to inspirational words, and other ways to boost a positive sales attitude will have the greatest impact when you do them on a daily basis and at about the same time. By disciplining yourself to engage in that activity, even when you're not in the mood, you will boost a sagging attitude and, in the process, raise up your sales.

P<u>art</u> II

Strategies to Help

Your Sales Team

Sell More to

Cautious Customers

Strategy 11

Build a Customer-Centric Sales Team

Salespeople who also provide outstanding customer service attract and keep more customers, especially when markets are down and customers are more cautious about spending their hard-earned dollars.
—Ron Volper Group 2010 Sales Study

Not long ago, I was running late to get to the hotel where I was to give a keynote speech for a new client in Chicago. As I was walking there, I noticed that the button on my left cuff had broken and the sleeve was caught in my suit jacket. I happened to be walking by a Nordstrom's department store at the time and rushed in to see if I could get a new white shirt. As I approached the men's department, a well-dressed young salesperson greeted me and asked, "How can I help you?"

I blurted out that I was on my way to give a speech, was running late, and needed a new shirt like the one I was wearing. He asked my size, showed me to a chair, and said, "Don't worry. Please have a seat and I'll be right back." Within a few minutes, the salesman returned with a new white dress shirt. He then practically took me by the arm to the men's dressing room and waited outside while I put it on. If I had let him, I think he would have buttoned it for me! He then escorted me over to the counter to pay for the shirt. At that point, he said something that I won't ever forget: "Would you like us to fix your other shirt and send it to you?"

"But I didn't buy it here and it's not one of yours," I gasped. He said it didn't matter. After I gave him my business card and thanked him, I went off to give my talk. When I returned to my office several days later, I noticed a package on my desk. When I opened the package, I found my old shirt, but, as promised, it had a new button on the sleeve and had been cleaned and pressed. Also in the package was a note from the salesperson saying it was a pleasure to work with me and that he hoped my speech had gone well. Talk about a pleasure to work with!

Salespeople Who Add Value Through Their Customer Service Increase Their Earnings

Most sales experts agree that salespeople who think and act beyond the sale by adding customer service to the benefits they provide their customers make more money. But there are also other downstream benefits to the salespeople, the sales managers, and the companies that use a customer-service approach to sales, including:

» Delighted customers.

» More repeat business.

» Customers' willingness to "buy up."

» Increase in customer referrals.

» Greater customer loyalty and lower customer attrition.

» Higher cross-sell ratios.

» Decrease in customer complaints.

» Decrease in length of the sales cycle.

» Increase in market share.

» More motivated salespeople and lower rep turnover.

» Better company image and greater pool of candidates to hire from.

Though a reputation for outstanding customer service helps companies attract and keep customers (and salespeople)

116

at any time, it can be especially powerful when markets are down and customers are more cautious about spending their hard-earned dollars, and demand more value from their purchase of your company's products or services.

The 3 Rs of a Customer Service–Oriented Salesperson

Sales managers need to make sure that their salespeople understand that customer service means: *the degree to which a salesperson and company meet and exceed customer expectations.* To meet and exceed customer expectations, I recommend that salespeople demonstrate what I call the 3Rs: *responsiveness, respect,* and *reliability.*

Responsiveness denotes how quickly salespeople provide customers with products or services relative to their expectations. Here is an example of a failure to meet customers' expectations regarding responsiveness. After launching a multi-million-dollar "Get Your Home Loan Approved Faster" advertising campaign, a regional bank in the Northeast ran into a major problem. The advertising campaign that showed happy customers emerging from the bank after being given big checks by friendly bankers (also known as salespeople) succeeded in attracting more customers to the branches, but the bank failed to hire enough staff to meet the expectations of their customers. Loans took far longer to process than the ad promised, leading to frustrated customers, many of whom ultimately left the bank—and took their money with them.

Respect is the degree to which salespeople demonstrate that they care about their customers. They demonstrate respect by words and deeds, but, of course, deeds are most important. Salespeople who interact with customers the most can easily show respect for them by returning phone calls promptly and by being mindful of their time.

Reliability is the degree to which salespeople recommend the right product or service to their customers and insure that it is implemented or installed in the right way. For example, if a rep for a telephone company recommends the best phone system for a small business, but it is not properly installed and some of the features don't work, then that rep would score poorly on reliability. Similarly, if a rep for a luxury hotel company recommends a beautiful ballroom for the company's annual meeting but the breakfast is served late, then that rep would also score low on reliability.

9 Ways Salespeople Exceed Customer Expectations Before the Sale

1. At the beginning of a sales call, hand customers a piece of paper with your proposed agenda for your meeting.

2. Ask customers how much time they have allotted for your sales call and, five minutes before that time, ask them if they would like you to wrap up or continue the discussion.

3. After your sales call, send customers a handwritten note thanking them for their time (and reminding them of the next step for both of you).

4. Return customer phone calls and e-mails the same day you receive them.

5. Under-promise and over-deliver, by completing proposals, reports, and so forth, before the promised date.

6. Give your customer an unsolicited referral for their business.

7. Take customers to a ball game, entertainment event, or fishing, golfing, or skiing, and don't say a word about business (unless they do).

8. Do something to help your customer's spouse or kids (find a job, a college, an apartment, a roommate, and so on).

9. Show customers you value their friendship by inviting them to a social event (such as birthday parties, holiday celebrations, and so forth).

9 Ways Salespeople Exceed Customer Expectations After the Sale

1. Give your customers your contact information, including your cell phone number, and encourage them to contact you at any time if they have any problems or questions.

2. Follow up a week or so after the sale to make sure that your customers are happy with their new product or service.

3. Ask your customers if they would like to complete a customer satisfaction survey.

4. Offer to be present the day your product arrives at your customers' premises or your service begins.

5. Have sales managers and other senior executives call customers and ask, "Do you have any suggestions on how we can improve our products or service?"

6. Ask your best customers if they would like to be part of a Customer Advisory Board with other senior executives to solicit their ideas about your company's products or services.

7. Ask your customers, "If we could change one thing about what we do and how we do it, what would that one thing be?"

8. Have the CEO and other senior executives regularly go on sales calls, and personally respond to letters of complaint and commendation from customers.

9. Personally handle all complaints, and follow up to make sure all issues are resolved in a timely fashion and to the customer's satisfaction.

Good News Travels Fast—Bad News Travels Faster

When its revenue was down, a major Midwestern bank tried to expand its business with middle-market companies without asking them about their expectations. To that end, it advertised that it would make commercial credit decisions in five weeks. Ironically, this bank, too, wound up with a net loss of customers because most CEOs, business owners, and professionals thought five weeks was too long to wait for a decision about a business loan. The lesson here, of course, is that instead of checking with their customers to learn their expectations, or at the very least, asking their salespeople about their customers' expectations, the bank made an assumption—in which they were dead wrong—about what their customers expected with regard to the time it should take to make a loan decision.

Instead of improving customer service, this bank simply talked about it. And for very different reasons, their customers talked about it, too. They talked about how long they had to wait for a decision and how no one at the bank seemed to care. Several studies indicate that customers who have a bad customer service experience tell between 10 and 13 people about it, and they, in turn, share it with others, so the negative publicity spreads rapidly. That's what happened to this bank. (And this was before the advent of social media, which can now spread customer complaints with a few clicks of a mouse.)

In consulting with executives in a range of industries, I often ask them what differentiates their company from its competitors. In the majority of cases, they cite customer service. Yet, further analysis reveals that their customer service is usually no better than their competitors', and sometimes even worse. So it seems that many sales managers, salespeople, and others say the right things about their company's customer service, but their companies are not doing much to improve it.

15 Ways to Build a Customer-Centric Company With Your Employees

1. Hire salespeople and customer contact people that care about other people and have demonstrated that in previous employment.

2. Base employee performance evaluations, compensation, and promotions in part on how responsive the person is to colleagues' requests.

3. Recognize and commend employees for going the extra mile for customers.

4. Provide salespeople and all customer contact staff with training in customer service skills, including how to handle irate customers.

5. Establish guidelines that empower salespeople and others to make certain decisions with regard to customer requests.

6. Encourage employees to offer suggestions to improve the customer experience.

7. Avoid berating salespeople and other employees when they make mistakes; instead use the situation, if appropriate, as a learning experience.

8. Talk about the importance of customer service as one of your company's core values and as a marketing strategy.

9. Coach employees at all levels on how to identify and meet customer expectations.

10. Hold employees accountable for resolving customer complaints.

11. Demonstrate a bias for actions, and solve underlying problems rather than just symptoms of problems.

12. Celebrate success in improving quality, or efficiency, or the overall customer experience.

13. Involve employees at all levels in quality teams. Teach managers and team leaders how to run them.

14. Create a communications program, via an e-newsletter or by other means, that keeps employees informed about the progress that various teams have made in identifying and solving company-wide and departmental problems.

15. Let it be known that customer service consists of doing many little things well, such as how quickly employees answer the phone and return phone calls, and how friendly they are on the phone to both external and internal customers.

A Customer Service Sales Culture Pays for Itself in Goodwill, Loyalty, and Profits

Creating a customer service sales culture is hard work and time-consuming, but most of the companies that have done so have more been successful in attracting and retaining customers (and salespeople), differentiating themselves from their competitors, gaining market share, and increasing profitability. And those things are worth working for.

Deliver Sales Training Programs That Add Revenue

The companies with the highest percentage of salespeople at or above their goals offer the most sales training...and the best sales training.
—Ron Volper Group 2010 Sales Study

Sam was one of 10 salespeople on my team when I was promoted to the position of sales manager for a Fortune 500 company that sold information services to other businesses. Sam was in her late 20s, bright, and hardworking, and she made more face-to-face sales calls than six of the other salespeople. Unfortunately, because Sam was only about halfway to her year-to-date goal, she was the team's lowest producer, and my predecessor was about to fire Sam after her fifth month in territory. As the new manager, I traveled with Sam and learned the following:

» She built good rapport with customers, and they enjoyed meeting with her.

» Sam was good at getting appointments, but she often failed to advance the sales process and close sales.

» Her prior sales experience consisted of retail selling in a small local appliance store.

When I asked Sam if she had ever received sales training she said, "Yes, some." In probing further, I learned that her "sales training" consisted of little more than the store owner standing over her for three hours telling her how to pitch the products and then giving her a three-ring binder describing the technical specifications of the appliances.

As it turned out, our team was scheduled the following week for a refresher course on *needs-based selling.* At this sales seminar, several things amazed me. Sam's level of enthusiasm and embracing of the sales concepts taught in the seminar was contagious. In fact, she was so involved in this seminar that she contributed even more than our top salespeople. The second, even more startling thing was that, after the seminar, she went on to become the second-highest producer among my team of veterans. When I asked her what she attributed her turnaround to, she said, "Learning how to question, overcome objections, and gaining customer commitment."

A Winning Sales Training Philosophy: Provide the Right Training at the Right Time

It was after this experience with Sam and several others like it, that as a sales manager and then VP of Sales, I learned the enormous value of sales training, but only if it is properly designed and implemented. It became clear to me that the right sales training at the right time was the most effective way to constantly increase revenue, prevent slumps, and help struggling salespeople like Sam win over cautious customers and become top performers. A focused and structured sales training program embedded the skills in salespeople's bones so that they used them in every sales call, and thus closed more deals.

Aligning Sales Training With Your Business Strategy

The most successful companies have a sales training strategy that is aligned with their marketing strategy and supportive of their business plan. That's why, as part of their sales strategy, and prior to implementing any sales training, senior executives brief the training director and human resources managers about their marketing vision and business goals for the year and longer-term.

The 3 Phases of Selling

The "before" sales skills typically consist of:

> Product knowledge.
> New business development: prospecting and qualifying.
> Territory management.

The "during" sales skills typically consist of:

> Needs-based selling.
> Sales presentations.
> Sales negotiations.

The "after" sales skills (or account management skills) typically consist of:

> Key account management.
> Time management.
> Cross-selling.

Identifying Your Team's and Team Members' Specific Training Needs

Once sales managers and training directors know their company's business strategy and plans, they can engage an outside consulting firm or personally conduct a comprehensive *needs analysis* of their sales team and an *individual performance analysis* of their team members. The results of these assessments culminate in individual and team sales training plans for all members of your team, including top performers, those who are struggling, and average producers. The specific skills, strategies, and techniques of your sales training program also depends upon your company's current sales process and sales culture.

Generic vs. Custom Sales Training: Which Is Better?

If the sales training presents the appropriate skills, does it matter whether it is generic or customized? Although generic products are useful to focus on selling skills rather than product knowledge, many salespeople—especially ones who are struggling in a down market—are less motivated to practice selling products that are not their own. For this reason, the best sales training programs are those that use the company's products, actual information about some of their accounts, specific sales scenarios, and role-playing exercises that address their cautious customers' needs and objections.

Using a Variety of Training Methods Makes for Effective Programs

Some companies attempt to teach sales skills using an on-line approach, but the most successful companies bring their team together for sales training in a seminar. On-line training can be efficient for product knowledge training and other informational training, but people learn selling skills and interpersonal communication skills most effectively with a face-to-face approach.

Make it Participative

The best sales training is highly interactive, allowing the participants to engage in a variety of activities on their own, with partners, in small groups of three to five, in medium groups of six to 10, and in the full group. Participative training includes having the attendees compare notes, brainstorm, and provide written and oral feedback to their partners and the full group.

Use Structured Role-Plays

Although some people are self-conscious or uncomfortable with role-playing, well-structured practice scenarios are a highly effective method of training that represent the nearest approximation a salesperson has to an actual sales situation. You can make role plays less daunting by dividing participants into groups of two or three and having them conduct role-plays in different locations, so they will not be disturbed by what others are saying or worry about what they may be thinking.

Use Relevant Case Studies

Choosing relevant case studies allows salespeople to identify and discuss skills, strategies, and other factors that relate to a specific sales situation. With case studies, you or an attendee can facilitate discussion, highlight critical issues, and ask attendees what they might do at any given point in the sales process.

Use Sales Games

Most salespeople are competitive by nature and usually enjoy engaging in learning games. To be effective, the games need to employ specific sales skills and problem-solving strategies that the salespeople can apply in real sales situations. For example, to encourage teamwork, you can divide people into teams and use a *Jeopardy* TV game show format (the contestants must come up with the question to a given answer) to reinforce product knowledge.

Use Oral Quizzes

Quizzes may not be thought of as much fun as other activities, but they can be made enjoyable, and can be used to reinforce and review sales concepts. To keep the tone light, sometimes I'll sprinkle in fun questions, such as "At our dinner last night, what was the waiter's name, or the special dessert on the menu?" I'll often award fun prizes to the participants, including the previous night's dessert.

Use Team Debates

Another effective training method is to set up a debate between two teams within the seminar. For example, I'll often pose sales question and ask people where they stand, *literally,* on the issue by asking them to walk to the side of the room that represents one opinion or another. For example, one question I use in my sales training is: "Where do you stand on this question? Is it a good idea to ask a customer what they *don't* like about the current product/service they are using."

Use a Skit, Song, or Story

Because many salespeople enjoy having fun (and being the center of attention), one of the ways to reinforce key skills and concepts is by breaking them into pairs or small groups and having them create a brief skit, or song, poem, or story that summarizes the key concepts. The team that most accurately captures the most seminar concepts (or gets the most applause!) receives a fun prize.

How Much Sales Training?

Though there are always exceptions, the companies that post the largest increases in sales revenues and capture the largest market share are the ones that usually provide their salespeople with approximately five days of structured sales and product knowledge training annually, whereas their less-successful competitors typically offer from zero days to one day of sales training. Depending upon which sales topics they teach, these best-performing companies typically implement the initial sales training program for two consecutive days, so that there is continuity for participants. The most effective sales training is typically presented in one- to three-hour modules where each skill or concept is part of a separate lesson to make it easier for participants to learn, practice, and integrate the skills. In addition, for salespeople who get promoted, receiving additional sales training prepares them for their new responsibilities. For example, a salesperson promoted to the position of key account manager would benefit from the seminar "Key Account Management."

Group Size and Composition

Although groups of three to five can certainly benefit from sales training, our studies show that the companies who have fewer salespeople who fall into slumps and who get out of slumps sooner are the ones that present sales training to groups of approximately eight to 15 so that the energy level stays high. They also use groups for the training that includes higher performers with lower performers, so that the weaker performers learn from their peers while the higher performers can further hone their sales skills and develop their training and leadership abilities.

Who Should Conduct the Sales Training?

Sales training can be conducted internally or by an outside consultant. The advantage of conducting it internally is that your internal trainer will know the culture of the company, and its policies, people, products, vision, and values better than most outside trainers, and may, as a result, have instant credibility with salespeople. The advantage of using an outside consultant is that, because the consultant has presumably worked with scores of other companies, she may have broader and deeper experience with sales and be able to bring in new ideas to expand your business.

9 Ways to Sabotage Sales Training

Regardless of who conducts the training, the trainer wins over the group—or fails to do so—by what she does prior to showing up almost as much as what she does during the actual seminar. I've seen too many seminars fall apart because of simple logistical issues, including the following:

1. Participants did not have correct information about where or when the seminar was being held, and did not arrive on time.
2. The leader did not have a leader's guide.

3. The leader failed to rehearse the seminar and did not satisfactorily explain how to do the seminar activities.

4. The leader failed to manage the group dynamics or got into a "power struggle" with one of the participants.

5. The group went off on a tangent and wasted a great deal of time.

6. The materials did not get to the right place (especially at a hotel or conference center).

7. The materials or equipment did not arrive or were not in working order.

8. The room was not set up prior to participants' arrival.

9. Participants were not properly informed about the seminar and did not complete, or bring the pre-work or the right materials or information to the seminar.

Measuring the Impact of Sales Training

Sales training is of no value unless it increases sales and/or sales efficiency—how long it takes a salesperson to seal a deal. Measurement encompasses two areas: the validity of the overall sales training program and the progress that each salesperson makes as a result of completing the training. Regarding validating the overall program, the first step is to ensure that the skills taught match the ones managers want salespeople to use as part of the sales process.

After checking that the program teaches the right skills, you'll want to ensure that participants are learning the skills and using them correctly in the seminar. The best way to do this is to sit in on the training, and satisfy yourself that all participants are following along and using the skills in practice activities, such as role-plays. Another way to assess progress during the seminar is to see how participants do on quizzes. Do they get the right answers? Are they asking relevant questions? The next level of validation is going on joint sales call with sales-people and seeing that the great majority are still using the sales skills—and using them correctly—with customers.

The most important validation—but the most challenging one to measure—is the impact the training has on sales revenues. One of the best ways to do this is to randomly divide the sales team into two groups (with an equal number of sales-people above quota, at quota, and below quota in each group). Have one group complete the training and measure whether their sales increase more than the control group, which does not experience the training. I recommend you track the two groups for three months. If you do see an increase, as you most often will if the training is well-designed, then you will want to conduct the training for the control group, too.

Each salesperson's progress can be tracked in a similar fashion. That is, you will want to see whether their sales increase after they have completed the sales training. Some of the sales outcomes you may want to track for each salesperson and for the entire sales team include increases in the following areas:

» Revenue from the previous quarter and from the same quarter in the previous year.
» Number of salespeople who meet and exceed their revenue goals.
» Number of accounts in their pipeline.
» Revenue per account.
» Cross-sales.
» Retention of accounts.
» Referrals from customers.

Effective Sales Training Methods Get Results

To be a top-performing company, your sales department must be committed to developing all the members of its sales team, from the top performers to those struggling to make their numbers. Whether you design your own sales training program or use an outside sales expert, be sure to align your sales training program with the goals and strategies of your company. Remember that when it comes to sales training, in most cases "one size does not fit all." Therefore, based on your team and individual assessments, use a variety of proven sales training methods to motivate all your team members to learn new skills, techniques, and strategies so they can win over cautious customers and increase their sales.

Strategy 13

Coach Your Team to Achieve Its Sales Goals

Top-performing salespeople agreed that the sales managers who coached them early in their careers helped them succeed.

—Ron Volper Group 2010 Sales Study

"Coaching is attracting America's top CEOs because, put simply, business coaching works. In fact, when asked for a conservative estimate of the monetary payoff from the coaching they got…managers described an average return of more than $100,000, or about six times what the coaching had cost their companies."

After reading this quote in *Fortune* magazine, I interviewed a variety of salespeople about their experiences being coached by their sales managers. Here is what I learned. Many top-performing salespeople said that the best sales managers were, in fact, devoted coaches who helped them develop their sales skills along with offering encouragement with balanced and unambiguous feedback. One salesperson told me, "I was lucky. My first sales manager was a great coach, too. She helped me discover strengths I didn't know I had, but she was tough. She coached me to be more self-reliant and showed me how to work my way out of sales slumps even when my customers were reluctant to buy."

However, interestingly, many of the less-productive salespeople that I asked about their coaching experiences offered a different opinion. Several had these similar views: "My sales manager keeps telling me I'm behind in my numbers and 'coaches' me to do better, but he has not helped me figure out why I'm behind. If that's what coaching is all about, count me out."

Pinpoint Areas for Improvement *Before* You Start Coaching

Top salespeople know that they need to first identify a customer's needs before they offer him or her any solutions or products. The same approach applies to sales managers when they prepare to coach their salespeople. The most successful sales managers use diagnostic tools to help them identify which areas the salesperson can improve in *before* they set up a formal coaching process—and they encourage the salesperson to participate in the analysis. The areas that most salespeople need coaching in are represented by letters in *K-A-S-H*:

K = Knowledge

Do your salespeople have adequate knowledge of both their customers and your company's products? For example, when I ran sales, I often asked my salespeople to tell me about their customers' customers. If they couldn't do so, I saw it as a red flag. Similarly, if the salesperson cannot draw an organization chart of the customer's company, it suggests that the salesperson doesn't understand the decision process at that company. Besides knowing about the company and its industry, knowledge means the salesperson knows the features, benefits, and applications of your company's products and services.

A = Attitude

If their market is down, even top-performing salespeople can succumb to negative thinking. For those salespeople in a slump or rookies having a tough time breaking into the business the right attitude plays an even more critical role. That is why salespeople who are engaging and funny are often able to get the most appointments and close more sales. In addition,

134

salespeople who have a sunny disposition don't take rejection personally and often make the most and the best sales calls. For example, in describing a call when she did not get the sale, even though she was disappointed, instead of saying "I lost the sale," one of my top sales executives told me that she had "a near success."

S = Skills

Effective sales managers not only can diagnose that the revenue shortfall may be related to a skill deficiency, but can pinpoint which specific sales skill the salesperson needs to strengthen. If your coaching efforts focus on one of the following skills, including building rapport, asking questions, overcoming objections, recommending solutions, gaining customers' commitment, giving sales presentations, delivering proposals, and developing new business, the salesperson will very likely increase his or her sales.

H = Habits

A salesperson's work habits refer to how well and how often she engages in sales-related activities. If you notice that a salesperson whose habits are usually productive suddenly changes and that change results in a lower level of performance, then look for the cause.

Caution: Don't Counsel Salespeople on Personal Issues

Though you want to show empathy in dealing with an employee with a personal problem, be careful not to cross the line and get involved in counseling the person about personal issues. Instead, refer them to a human resources representative in your company.

Communication, Belief, Motivation, and Obstacles

As a top-performing salesperson and VP of sales, I added *communication, belief, motivation,* and *obstacles* to this list of areas that respond to coaching.

Communication

Let's say one of your salespeople has not brought in any new business in a given quarter. Though developing new business seems to be an obvious part of a salesperson's job, it's entirely possible that she did not know this is important to the company, and if you have not specifically mentioned this to your sales team and incorporated new business into their goals, then the communications breakdown is not entirely her fault. If you want to get your message through to your salespeople (many of whom are "running and gunning" and some of whom may have a short attention span), then you need to communicate it repeatedly. The point where you're tired of saying it, is often the point when your salespeople finally get the message. Coaching can improve the communication between sales managers and their salespeople.

Belief

Many years ago (when most banks were not sales-driven), I consulted with a number of major banks that wanted to build a sales culture and train their bankers to proactively cross-sell their products. In several cases, they received pushback from the bankers. Some of the bankers protested, "It is undignified for a bank to push products on customers." Although this was not what senior management was attempting to do, the resistance these bankers showed stemmed from their belief that customers would resent it. Coaching can correct a misinterpretation of belief between sales managers and their team.

Motivation

What motivates your salespeople? Is it money, recognition, authority, status, your approval—maybe all these and more? Because personal motivation often differs between members of your team, you need to determine first why a salesperson does or doesn't do something that affects his or her sales performance. Motivation is directly related to personal benefit, and thus to commitment. Most salespeople need to see the payoff of what you want them to do before they feel motivated enough to make a commitment to the task. Once you know the person's source of motivation, then you can use coaching to address issues or to encourage or discourage specific behaviors.

Obstacles

Some struggling salespeople who can benefit from your coaching might point to factors that prevent them from doing what you want them to do. For example, I consulted with a bank executive whose bankers resisted cross-selling to other customers. They were responsible for doing a credit analysis of customers requesting loans, and they pointed out that, with their new responsibilities, they simply did not have the time to go out in the field and engage in selling. In this case, the manager needed to first address and resolve this obstacle.

11 Coaching Tips to Motivate and Support Your Sales Team

1. Use Different Coaching Formats

Top-performing sales managers can coach their salespeople during in-person sales calls and sales calls via the telephone using the following three formats: (1) Listen, Observe, and Feedback, (2) Sales Modeling Call, and (3) Spot Coaching.

Listen, Observe, and Feedback

Before you meet a customer, be sure to discuss with the salesperson what your respective roles will be during the time you are on the sales call. After you, your salesperson, and the customer exchange your greetings, take a back seat and say as little as possible. The only exception to this is if the salesperson flounders or asks for your opinion, or says something that is egregiously wrong and needs to be immediately corrected.

Sales Modeling Call

Modeling is a demonstration by the sales manager of the sales process or a part of it, and is most appropriate for new salespeople or those who are struggling to make their numbers.

For example, if your salesperson is uncomfortable handling objections, you might conduct all or a part of the sales call to show him how you do it.

Spot Coaching

Another type of coaching is called *spot coaching,* also known as spontaneous coaching. Spot coaching is appropriate if you overhear a salesperson on the phone or in a face-to-face sales call say something that is factually incorrect. For example, if a salesperson quotes the wrong price to a customer, you can use spot coaching to correct her, but you do not want to embarrass the salesperson in front of the customer or her peers. Wait until she concludes the conversation, and then take her aside and offer spot coaching on how to inform the customer of her mistake.

Caution: Don't Coach if You Are on a Joint Sales Call

I urge you *not* to coach a salesperson after a joint sales call. If you're making a joint sales call to a buying committee, for example, you and your salesperson must decide ahead of time on your respective roles during the meeting. However, there are far too many dynamics at play in the sales call for you to objectively coach the salesperson.

2. Never Kick Your Salespeople When They're Down

One reason some salespeople have a negative attitude toward coaching is that some sales managers spend much of their coaching time telling salespeople that their results are unsatisfactory, and directly or indirectly threatening them with dire consequences if they don't improve. With few exceptions, salespeople know their numbers and, if they are below goal, they are plenty worried about paying their bills or even losing their job. All this threat accomplishes is to further inflame their anxiety and make them press their customers for a sale in a way that makes customers uncomfortable and less likely to buy from them.

Skilled coaches do the opposite. Though they won't sugar-coat the truth, they will express confidence in the salesperson and pump him up rather than bring him down. For example, instead of saying, "You're numbers are totally unacceptable," they might say, "Thinking about how well you've done in the past, we're both disappointed with your numbers this quarter. Let's talk about what you can do and what I can do to help you get back on track."

3. Stay Positive Even if a Salesperson Has a Bad Month

One of the mistakes some sales managers make is that they attach too much importance to a given set of sales figures. The numbers are important, but only if you interpret them in context by looking at trends and comparisons. For example, if a salesperson does not achieve his revenue goal for the current month, but has significantly increased his sales revenues for each of the last three months, that is a positive trend.

4. Spend Time in the Field With Your Salespeople

Coaches who are successful look at the numbers for both results and activities. But even more importantly, they look behind the numbers to determine why the salesperson's results may not be up to par. Though the numbers are important as a starting point, top-performing sales managers spend time out in the field with their salespeople to observe firsthand what they are doing and why. A top sales manager knows that she can't base her diagnosis on one or even two sales calls. Instead, she'll spend a full day making calls with the salesperson.

5. Create a Coaching Plan for the Salesperson

After doing the diagnosis, I find it helpful to create a simple, one-page coaching plan describing the area I believe each salesperson could be better at, and detailing a coaching plan for that salesperson. By reducing the plan to writing, you formalize what needs to happen and by when, and you reduce misunderstandings. In some ways the coaching plan is like an account plan that a salesperson might put together for a high potential account. It lists key goals and time lines, and also delineates what the salesperson will do to enhance his performance and what you as the manager will do to support the salesperson.

6. Remember the Goals of a Coaching Discussion

There are three goals in a coaching discussion with a salesperson. Your first goal is to have the salesperson agree with you that she can improve in a specific area of sales. (But be open to the possibility that you may be wrong in your diagnosis.) The second objective of a focused coaching session is to get the salesperson to agree with you on a specific action plan to make the improvement. The third objective is to begin and end the discussion in a way that the salesperson feels good about herself, and sees you the sales manager as an ally and trusted advisor.

7. Use the Ham Sandwich Method When Coaching Salespeople

Most salespeople enjoy hearing praise from their sales manager, but can become defensive when they hear critical comments. Top sales managers deliver both praise and constructive criticism to a salesperson by using what I call the "ham sandwich method" when they offer feedback. First, they say something encouraging and positive about the salesperson's results or activities, then they point out (or guide the salesperson to articulate) an area for improvement, and finally they conclude the analysis with another positive. The two slices of bread represent the two positive statements, and the ham in the center of the sandwich represents the constructive criticism.

8. Use Sales Skills to Win Over Salespeople

As mentioned, a sales manager can only successfully coach salespeople if the manager diagnoses the precise reason(s) for any revenue shortfall. However, that is not enough. The sales manager must also be able to gain the trust of salespeople and have them agree with your diagnosis and recommended plan of action. The sales managers who have established the best relationships with their salespeople are the ones who think of their salespeople as customers, and use the same sales skills with them that they want them to use with their customers. These communication skills consist of:

» Establishing rapport with salespeople.

» Identifying needs by asking questions and by observing sales calls.

» Making benefits-centered recommendations to the salespeople to enhance their performance.

» Overcoming any objections from salespeople.

» Gaining their commitment to a course of action.

9. Create a Coaching Schedule

As a sales manager, I found it helpful to create a coaching schedule each month, so I could apportion my time appropriately. I reminded myself that in my first management position my title was field sales manager, so I spent as much time as possible traveling with and coaching each salesperson. My goal was to be with each salesperson once a month. Of course, the schedule changed based on emerging sales opportunities, but it gave my sales team and me a track to run on, and my team felt better knowing my schedule in advance, so they could plan their sales calls accordingly.

10. Don't Ignore Your Star Performers

One of the mistakes newly promoted and even veteran sales managers make is that they spend all of their time coaching the weaker performers and ignore their star salespeople.

141

Assuming you have an equal number of salespeople who are stars, satisfactory, and sub-standard, I suggest that you spend approximately 40 percent of your time with the low performers, 40 percent of your time with the satisfactory performers, and 20 percent with the stars.

With regard to the stars, some of them can progress to the next level and become superstars. It's worth remembering that even superstar baseball players strike out a lot more often than they get on base, so there's always room for improvement. Besides that, you will pick up a few sales strategies from them that you can share with the other members of your team. And the sales stars will enjoy hearing you compliment them on their virtuoso performances.

11. Encourage Peer Coaching

One of the practices I learned from my first sales manager when I was a salesperson was to encourage salespeople to go on calls with each other and coach their peers. There are four benefits of peer coaching. This often works well because salespeople are less threatened and less defensive if they hear suggestions from a peer instead of their boss; they don't feel they are being judged in the same way. The second benefit is that usually both salespeople learn from observing each other. The third benefit is that it is a way to prepare a star salesperson for the role of sales manager. The fourth is that some customers feel flattered and important when more than one person from the same company calls on them.

Effective Coaching Helps Create a Top-Performing Sales Team

By coaching everyone on your team, including sales assistants and others, you communicate that coaching is a positive activity, and that everyone can grow and improve. And most people will. In the best-managed companies, not only the salespeople but the managers are coached by their managers, so the coaching becomes embedded into the fabric of the organization. My experience suggests, however, that even though most people can improve their performance, some salespeople are simply not right for the job. In this case, the answer is not to increase your coaching, but (after you have taken all the appropriate actions) to let them know. Moreover, though most salespeople don't get enough time with their manager, you don't want to overwhelm salespeople by constantly breathing down their necks.

Because sales managers wear many hats, including that of disciplinarian, salespeople are sometimes wary of being coached and may hear any criticism as threatening or even career-ending. The truth, however, is that, when the manager correctly identifies the issues and uses consultative sales skills to make suggestions, she is giving her salespeople a gift—one that will result in greater success for them throughout their career.

Strategy 14

Make Every Sales Meeting Increase Your Team's Productivity

Sales meetings that actively involve the salespeople have a positive impact not only on the perceived value of the meeting, but also on sales revenues.

—Ron Volper Group 2010 Sales Study

Last year the VP of business development of a global consulting firm called me with this desperate plea: "Ron, you've got to help me! When it comes to face-to-face sales, I close lots of business, but my monthly sales meetings are a disaster! When I'm speaking to our salespeople at our sales meetings, half are on their cell phones texting or engaged in side conversations! I'm lucky if the other half in the room actually listen to what I'm saying. I'm about ready to chuck these meetings altogether!"

If this complaint sounds familiar, then the results from my follow-up questionnaire to his team will also come as no surprise: "The meeting was a complete waste of time." "I didn't learn anything at his meeting." "It was a bad use of my time." "I have no idea what the purpose of the meeting was." "He could have sent an e-mail instead of having a meeting." "He's a great guy and helpful when we're out in the field, but his meetings are a waste of time."

Although negative comments about sales meetings are nothing new, you don't have to accept them as a fact of life.

On the contrary, sales meetings can offer a great opportunity for top sales managers to motivate and lead their teams to win over cautious customers in a down market—and it's easier than you might think. Here's how you can use your sales meetings as a powerful sales and management tool.

5 Criteria of Effective Sales Meetings

There are two types of meetings: regularly scheduled sales meetings, such as a weekly meeting to review the sales forecasts, and specially scheduled meetings, such as one to launch a new product. Specially held sales meetings are often more elaborate and more costly, but most of the elements of a successful meeting apply whether you are conducting a regularly scheduled, recurring meeting or a specially scheduled one. Top sales managers who conduct effective sales meeting apply these criteria:

» They define clear meeting objectives and set an agenda.

» They require a minimum amount of time and stick to their agenda.

» They encourage attendees to participate in a wide range of activities during the meeting.

» They check that the attendees feel good about the process.

» They make sure that the meeting contributes to increased sales.

Setting Your Meeting Objectives

Why are you having the meeting? What do you want to accomplish? The direct and indirect costs of meetings, and the time involved in planning and holding them are substantial, so make sure a meeting is in fact the best vehicle to achieve your objectives. For this reason, I recommend that you consider your desired outcomes of the meeting as you plan it. Effective sales meetings help salespeople make more and better sales, by doing one or more of the following:

» Providing them with useful and timely information.

» Brainstorming solutions to sales problems.

» Enhancing salespeople's skills.

» Motivating them to sell more.

» Making a decision.

» Establishing sales plans.

As you clarify your meeting's objectives, also define what actions you want to see your sales team take as a result of the meeting. For example, if your objective is to introduce a new product to your sales team, specific actions you might want your team to take might be to:

» Get excited about the new product.

» Learn the information they need to sell it.

» Brainstorm various benefits of the new product.

» Resolve any concerns they might have about selling in a down market (such as how to position it against other products your company offers and how to sell it against the competition).

» Practice overcoming objections from cautious customers.

» Plan how to incorporate this new product into their existing line.

When *Not* to Hold a Meeting

If you can convey the information better via an e-mail, memo, or a telephone conference call, then skip the meeting. Holding an unnecessary meeting only dilutes the value of future meetings and erodes your credibility.

17 Questions to Answer Before, During, and After Your Sales Meeting

Before Your Meeting

1. How will you plan and set your agenda?

Most top-performing sales managers agree with the old saw "time is money." As a result, they set meeting agendas that prioritize the items they wish to cover, the order in which they will discuss them, and a time limit for each topic. They often will distribute the proposed agenda several days before the meeting, and ask for feedback and suggestions for additional items. Then they hand out the final agenda at the meeting.

2. Where and when will you hold the meeting?

I have been at too many meetings where the assigned room was not available. One of the more embarrassing things that can happen is to have the group traipsing around looking for a meeting space at the last minute. Instead, be sure you book the room in advance and confirm its availability before your meeting. Though it is less costly and more time-efficient to hold meetings at your company offices, holding meetings off-site can stimulate fresh thinking and signal their importance. Off-site meetings can also reduce interruptions and distractions that often plague attendees at on-site meetings. Ideally you should vary the venue for your meetings. Also consider holding your meetings at times that are less disruptive or inconvenient to the attendees. One alternative for the many salespeople who are unable to attend a meeting in person because they are traveling is to attend virtually via GoToMeeting, Skype, and other communication tools.

3. How long will your meeting last?

Most salespeople prefer sales meetings that last less than an hour. If you set aside a certain amount of time for an item on the agenda, do not exceed the allotted time. If necessary, assign an item that needs more time to a small group or revisit it at a future meeting, but do not let it take time away from other items on the agenda.

4. How will you get people to arrive on time?

Top-performing sales managers start and end their meetings on time, and often use e-mails or various software programs to notify and remind people of scheduled meetings and that it will start and end on time. By starting and ending meetings on time, not only do you discourage late-comers, your sales team can more effectively plan their other sales activities. Never penalize people who arrive on time by waiting for latecomers.

5. How will you arrange the seating?

The seating configuration should flow from the size and shape of the meeting room and the purpose of your meeting. For example, if you're trying to stimulate brainstorming or small-group activity, or maximize discussion, arrange the seats in a U-shape. If you have round tables and you will be presenting information from the front of the room, it's better to have all chairs at each table facing the front of the room.

6. What materials or equipment will you use during the meeting?

Think through what items you will use during the meeting and when you will distribute them. For example, at several of my meetings, I put together mini-case studies and used them to facilitate discussion about sales strategy and tactics.

7. What reading or work can salespeople complete beforehand?

You can save time and make the meeting more effective by asking people to read documents or prepare certain information prior to the meeting. Doing this not only conveys to salespeople that you have given thought to the meeting, but focuses them on the meeting's objectives and their role.

8. What are your expectations for attendees' behavior at the meeting?

Are your meetings organized and controlled, or chaotic and unfocused? As a sales leader, you are responsible for establishing the atmosphere of the meeting. This is particularly important for setting the tone and your expectations for new team members. Therefore, it is worth taking a few minutes *prior* to one of your meetings to establish ground rules for meeting behavior by distributing a brief set of "meeting guidelines" via e-mail. These guidelines should include requesting that during the meeting, attendees:

» Refrain from texting or talking on cell phones.

» Give other team members their full attention.

» Avoid side conversations and interruptions.

» Participate with questions and constructive suggestions.

If there are a few people in the group who typically engage in distracting or troublesome behavior during your meetings, extending your request in person ahead of time and getting them more involved in the presentation usually solves the problem.

During the Meeting

9. How will you open the meeting and establish an upbeat atmosphere?

It's helpful to get participants' attention right off the bat. Sometimes reading an inspirational poem, citing a relevant news article, or sharing a personal experience works. What's important is that, as the leader, you talk from the heart. As part of your agenda, take a few minutes

149

to offer congratulations to team members who have had recent successes. Congratulate as many people as you legitimately can for closing specific deals and for overall revenue results, for sale of specific products, for increased sales activity, and even for forecasting accuracy. Thank people on your team for undertaking special projects.

Provide a few extra minutes and an opportunity for team members to shine by having a few of them talk about their recent sales successes and how they achieved them. The purpose of this activity is two-fold: to give salespeople the attention they deserve (and that many crave) for their success, and also to help others by sharing what worked for them in a down market. Ask top-performing salespeople to talk about how they uncovered the opportunity and the specific actions they took to bring in and close a large piece of business. Ask them:

» Who were the key players?

» What were the companies and key players' needs and expectations?

» What obstacles did you encounter and how did you overcome them?

» Who was the competition and how did you win against them?

» What were the key events in the sales cycle?

» Who else on the team helped you to close the deal?

» What are the next steps, and what is the long-term potential of this account?

» What were the key lessons you learned from this win?

10. How will you make your sales meeting interesting?

Inviting a special guest is one of the best ways to keep your sales meetings interesting. The best meetings I conducted were the ones where I invited customers to join us.

Customers said they often felt honored to be invited to our meetings, and our salespeople learned a great deal from their candid comments about what they expect from salespeople and their companies. For example, at one meeting, I invited a few customers to judge which salespeople gave the best presentations on our products. At another sales meeting, which focused on overcoming customer objections, I asked a favorite customer of mine to play the part of a cautious customer in a practice role play.

11. How will you facilitate participation?

When I was a VP of sales, my most productive meetings took place when I assigned roles to as many people as possible several days prior to the meeting—and not just to the top-performing salespeople. I rotated these roles between sales rookies, average performers, and even salespeople in a slump so everyone on the team at one time or another would have an opportunity to shine before their peers. Here are a few ways to encourage participation:

» Have your sales team identify recent sales situations, brainstorm strategies to win over cautious customers, and role-play solutions. Your sales meeting presents a huge opportunity for all your sales team to identify current challenges and objections from cautious customers, and come up with practical solutions that can lead to more sales. Add this 15-minute activity to your agenda. As a group, identify several specific sales challenges related to cautious customers in down markets. Then break into groups of two to five people to brainstorm solutions for five minutes. Next, ask each group to choose two people to briefly play the situation. Finally, elicit feedback from the group.

» Ask your sales team for ideas before you make decisions that affect them. "I would have been happy to share my ideas, but no one bothered to ask me" is a familiar complaint you hear from salespeople. Sales meetings can also be a good opportunity to solicit salespeople's ideas. For example, before making a final decision on the incentive compensation plan for my sales team, I always solicit their input. I ask them what they like and don't like about the current plan. The caveat to this is that you need to make it clear that you and the management team reserve the right to make the final decision about things such as the incentive compensation plan.

12. How will you handle under-involved and over-involved participants?

If you know a salesperson tends not to talk at meetings, you can assign him a topic to lead. Or you can ask a question and call on him to respond, especially if it's a question of opinion rather than fact. Be certain that you have an action plan for as many items as possible, with the exception of pure informational items. Make note of who will do what by when and what progress checks there will be. Assign someone to take the minutes and record key decisions and actions.

With over-involved people, one strategy is not to look at them as they are asking to be recognized. Another is to say, "Joe, you've already given us some good ideas. I want to hear from others." If some individuals are consistently under- or over-involved at meetings, it often helps to talk to them beforehand, and in a supportive way, ask them to modify their level of involvement at the meeting.

13. How can you boost the morale of slumping salespeople?

A sales meeting is a good venue to raise the spirits of the whole team, but it's especially a good opportunity to pump up salespeople who may be in a slump. The way to do this is two-fold:

First, give them an opportunity to conduct a portion of the meeting, especially if it's in an area of their demonstrated strength. For example, if you're facing competitive challenges, have them be responsible for coordinating the delivery of information about key competitors.

A second way is to compliment them publicly on some achievement or contribution to the sales team or the overall company. Although you're ultimately looking for revenue results and for every person on the team to exceed his or her quota, it's worthwhile to compliment people who have not yet hit their revenue target for an increase in activity (such as the number of sales calls made over a given period) or for closing an important account against the competition. It's also good to acknowledge their contribution to helping with such things that might come under the heading of corporate citizenship (helping coordinate the blood drive, the company picnic, or the holiday party). The idea is to find a legitimate reason for recognizing them, so they'll feel up when their sales are down.

14. How will you handle topics not on the agenda?

If an attendee raises an issue not on the agenda or one that is off the topics planned for discussion, don't feel obligated to discuss it at the time. You are usually better off making a note of it and addressing it at a subsequent meeting. If you have a flip chart available label a sheet "Parking Lot" and list extraneous items on it. Similarly, if a person raises an issue that only concerns him or her, then discuss it after the meeting is over.

15. How will you close the meeting?

Close your meeting on a positive note by thanking participants for their time and participation. Summarize the most important points or decisions. Before you say good-bye, remind the attendees of their action steps.

After the Meeting

16. How will you evaluate the success of the meeting?

Once your meeting concludes, you can ask key members of your team to remain for a few minutes to discuss what they think worked well at the meeting, what didn't, and what changes in the format or content they would like for the next meeting. Encourage them to be open and honest in their verbal or written evaluations.

17. How will you follow up on attendee assignments, actions, and decisions?

Top-performing sales managers know that when and how they follow up with attendees after the meeting plays a critical role if they are to achieve their sales objectives. When is the best time to follow up? Most agree to make your next contact with the attendees within a few days, but no longer than a week. You can follow up with:

» An answer to a question you couldn't address in the meeting.

» Feedback on an attendee's idea that you didn't get a chance to respond to.

» A specific issue that you or the attendee wish to privately discuss.

» A progress check to see if attendees understood their assignments.

Effective Sales Meetings Build Cohesive Teams That Lead to More Sales

Aristotle's observation that "The whole is **greater than the sum of its parts**" certainly applies when a top-performing sales manager runs a great sales meeting. In addition to the many other benefits, a focused, interactive, and practical sales meeting builds a top-performing team that will make more sales in a down market.

Strategy 15

Recruit and Hire Top Producers for Your Sales Team

Companies that have the lowest turnover of salespeople put sales candidates through the most interviews before hiring them.

—Ron Volper Group 2010 Sales Study

"Ron, I need someone to fill my top sales position right away or I'll be in big trouble!"

It couldn't have been a worse time for my client to find a suitable replacement for her number-one salesperson. My client's customers were high-end and extremely demanding. To make matters worse, my client's projected annual sales were based on the usual high revenues generated by her now-departed top salesperson! On top of this, many of the salespeople's markets were down.

Waiting until a vacancy occurs before beginning the hiring process is probably the worst possible time to start recruiting a replacement, but it's a common mistake that even some seasoned sales managers make. If they are under pressure to immediately fill an open territory, there is a greater chance that it will lead to a bad hire and a lot of collateral damage, including lost revenues, neglected customers, high turnover, low morale—and a big headache for you, the sales manager!

Recruiting and hiring the right salespeople is one of the most important parts of a sales manager's job. Yet, according to our survey, even experienced sales managers hire reps approximately 25 percent of the time who don't make their numbers or leave the company within a year of taking a sales position.

4-Step Approach to Recruiting and Hiring the Best Salespeople

Step 1: Take a proactive approach and do succession planning.

Step 2: Analyze and define the position *before* beginning your candidate search.

Step 3: Keep your candidate pipeline filled with competent job-seekers.

Step 4: Assess candidates' strategies for dealing with challenging sales situations.

Step 1: Take a Proactive Approach and Do Succession Planning

The smartest sales managers prevent themselves from being blindsided by an unanticipated turnover by doing succession planning. That means they forecast the likelihood that one of their salespeople (or any other person supporting them, such as a sales assistant) might leave. Savvy managers do this regardless of how well their team is producing, but pay special attention to anticipating turnover of salespeople when markets are down, because more salespeople may be struggling and getting discouraged.

The succession planning process works as follows. First, the manager holds a candid conversation with salespeople at least twice a year to discuss their aspirations and how they feel about their current positions. Then, based on the discussion and other information about each salesperson's results and activity level, the manager forecasts the probability of each salesperson staying, quitting, getting promoted, or being fired on a scale of 1–5 (5 means the person has announced his or her resignation; 1 means there is very little likelihood of the person's leaving).

156

For example, a salesperson that is consistently below his numbers and has been put on a performance improvement plan would most likely be rated a 4. However, salespeople forecasted to leave are not only the ones who are struggling. A salesperson might vacate the territory because he is likely to be promoted or because your company pays appreciably less than others in your industry, and you know he has interviewed with other companies.

Although some managers might feel uncomfortable having this discussion, it can be helpful for the salesperson, because she gets to share her career goals with her manager and ideally receives advice about what she can do to prepare herself to be promoted to the next position.

For each person on the team, the sales manager delineates in writing a specific strategy to fill the anticipated vacancy. Usually this means hiring a replacement, but it can also mean splitting the territory among other salespeople. In some cases, the manager may have a short-term strategy to cover the territory, plus a longer-term strategy. Keep in mind that if you split the territory as a short-term strategy, make sure that your salespeople understand that they will have to relinquish these accounts once you hire a full-time replacement.

Step 2: Analyze and Define the Position Before Beginning Your Candidate Search

Before you start searching for candidates, you first need to analyze and define the sales position. However, one of the common mistakes managers make in hiring salespeople is their failure to first define the specific responsibilities that the job entails and then the required competencies. Following are some of the key questions to consider in writing the job description and competencies for a sales position:

» Is the salesperson's primary responsibility to manage existing relationships and accounts (a farmer) or to develop new ones (a hunter)?

» Is the sales cycle long and complex, or is the sale more of a transaction?

» How much support in the form of leads, marketing literature, advertising, and such does the company provide?

» How knowledgeable about the product or industry must the salesperson be?

» Are the customers and products highly technical, and will the salesperson be engaged in technical discussions?

» Who are the salesperson's customers: C-level executives, middle managers, purchasing agents?

» How much after-sale support is expected from the salesperson?

» How well-known is the company versus its competitors?

» How well-known is the brand?

» How intense is the competition in this industry?

» How will the salesperson be measured?

» Will the salesperson be required to write proposals?

» Will the salesperson be selling a new concept or a new product, or a known commodity product?

» How much overnight travel is required?

» Will the salesperson be part of a sales team or be autonomous?

» Will the salesperson be required to give stand-up presentations to buying committees?

Step 3: Keep Your Candidate Pipeline Filled With Competent Job-Seekers

Once you have analyzed and defined the sales position, you are ready to actively seek the best candidates. Although there are many ways to go about recruiting and hiring salespeople, some work better than others. The following "best recruiting practices" will sharpen your efforts to fill sales vacancies with the right candidates.

Keep Your Net in the Water

The most successful managers always interview salespeople—and especially star salespeople—even when there is no open territory. They find out who the top salespeople in their industry (and related industries) are and proactively nurture those relationships. By inviting a top salesperson from a competitor to breakfast, the salesperson will usually be flattered, and you as the manager will gain valuable information.

Create a Farm Team Within Your Sales Organization

One strategy directly related to succession planning is to create a "farm team" of upcoming sales reps, just as they do in the major leagues in baseball. You want to have available high-potential players who you can mold into superstars. One way to do this is to hire bright, highly motivated young people with great potential, but limited sales experience. If your budget allows, you can have them work as sales assistants (junior salespeople) with some of your top salespeople, and also assign them a very limited number of accounts. While they are doing this, you and one or more of your salespeople can coach them so they realize their potential as soon as possible. For example, my firm hired a sales assistant who called new leads to qualify them and helped set up appointments for the senior sales reps. Within a few years, he was promoted to a senior sales position and went on to become one of our highest-earning salespeople.

Enlist the Help of Your Coworkers, Colleagues, Customers, Suppliers, Friends, and Family

One of the best ways to identify sales talent is to enlist the help of others. Although it would be great if your colleagues did this as good corporate citizens, the reality is that unless they have a compelling reason for doing so, most people are too busy to think about anything beyond their own job

159

responsibilities. For this reason, I recommend that you offer any non-management employee of your company a finder's fee for any candidate that he or she recommends and the company hires. One of my previous employers gave a $1,000 finder's fee to anyone who referred a candidate who the company hired, and wound up with a sales team that was able to win over cautious customers that our competitors had stopped calling on. Besides that, post positions on your company bulletin board, newsletter, and Website.

A related strategy is to get the word out to your customers, suppliers, friends, and family, so they, too, can refer sales candidates. In a down market, with many people looking for work, the challenge is that you may have too many applicants—not too few.

Attract Candidates by Establishing a High Profile in Your Industry

Top sales managers who have a high profile in their industry by addressing industry gatherings, writing articles, and assuming leadership positions in associations and other business venues will attract top salespeople. Adopting a high profile allows them to spot, meet, and entice talented salespeople who are always looking for better opportunities to make more money. For example, because I accepted an adjunct faculty appointment at a leading university, several years later, I was able to hire a talented graduate student who had been a student in one of my classes. More recently, I gave a talk to the business club of a well-known university and received resumes from several outstanding graduate students.

Advertise on Career and Employment Websites for Entry-Level and Mid-Level Sales Positions

Before the advent of employment and career Websites such as Monster.com, most salespeople looked for jobs in the "Sales Positions Offered" section in the classified ads of their local newspaper. If the salesperson found a possible job, he or she would send the employer a resume with a cover letter and wait to be called for an interview. Since then, however, online job classified ads have become the most popular way for employers to advertise sales jobs, and for job-seekers to find and apply for available sales positions.

Use Social Media to Pre-Screen and Qualify the Sales Candidates

Social media such as LinkedIn and Facebook are effective and popular ways for sales managers to reach and review large pools of job candidates before meeting face-to-face or even talking to them on the telephone. For example, on LinkedIn sales managers can read an applicant's profile that includes employment history, education, professional affiliations—even recommendations and possible mutual contacts. With Facebook, for example, you can initiate on-line conversations about sales-related topics in one of the many popular business chat rooms. Savvy sales managers know that an informal on-line conversation can reveal a great deal about a salesperson's approach to sales, customer service, and product knowledge. Once you have met a salesperson in a chat room who may be interested in exploring a new position at your company, you can extend an invitation to have a private conversation on-line, on the telephone, or in person to discuss it further.

Use a Sales Aptitude Questionnaire to Determine Sales Competencies

Once you find a job candidate with an impressive resume, appealing online profile, or notable referral, consider taking one more step before you commit to time-consuming face-to-face interviews. Remember that even the most experienced sales managers make wrong hiring decisions. One way to help reduce this kind of staffing mistake, particularly with new hires or those transitioning into sales from another profession, is by giving them a standardized sales aptitude questionnaire. Most sales aptitude questionnaires help sales managers determine if a candidate has the potential to succeed in a relationship-driven sales position that requires the following competencies:

» Driven.

» Competitive.

» Self-starter.

» Organized.

» Persistent.

» Optimistic.

Note that for a veteran salesperson with a proven track record, standardized sales aptitude questionnaires are usually unnecessary—or even a turnoff—so use them judiciously.

Step 4: Assess Candidates' Strategies for Dealing With Challenging Sales Situations

Face-to-face interviews are where sales managers have the best opportunity to assess a candidate's suitability for a sales position and how well the candidate fits into the culture of your company and sales organization. In addition to explaining sales activities, responsibilities, and the conditions under which the salesperson will work, discuss the vision and values of your company.

Past Performance Is the Best Predictor of Future Success

Once you've defined the job responsibilities and conditions of employment, you'll want to hone in on the candidates' background and experience to see how well they are aligned with your requirements. In their advertisements, financial services firms include the disclaimer that past performance does not guarantee future success. That's true with regard to investments and it's true with regard to job performance. However, past success in sales is an excellent indicator of the likelihood of future success. That is why you want to be sure that the applicant is not just engaging in "interview behavior" (telling you what she thinks you want to hear) and has really done what she claims to have done—and ideally has done it in an environment that parallels that in your company. For example, a salesperson who was successful in selling for a Fortune 1000 company that provided a great deal of support and structure may find it difficult to sell for a small, privately held company that may offer less of both. You'll want to explore this with the applicant.

Most job interviews fail to produce sufficient evidence upon which to make a sound hiring decision for several reasons. First, many interviewers do not study the candidate's resume sufficiently to prepare in-depth questions or probe deeply enough. Second, not enough people interview the candidate, and those who do often neglect to coordinate their interview strategy or the questions they ask and the answers they seek. Finally, interviewers often neglect to compare notes after the interview.

If you're looking to hire a candidate in a tough economy, look for evidence of how she dealt with other challenges from the economy and from other areas of life. Let's say that the applicant claims to be the top salesperson in her company. Most interviewers would congratulate her, ask a few questions about that, and then move on to other areas of her resume. However, a savvy sales manager would explore that claim in depth, plus ask questions that relate to the challenges of the open position, including that of dealing with more cautious customers.

Sample Interview Questions About a Candidate's Prior Successes

> *Congratulations on being the top salesperson in your company. Can you tell me how you did it?*

> *Describe for me your best sale in the past year. How much was it for, and what was your biggest challenge in closing the deal?*

> *What was your customer like, and what was your strategy going into the sale?*

> *What aspect of your strategy worked the best?*

> ❧ *What approaches didn't work as well as you had hoped, and how did you adapt?*

> ❧ *If you could pinpoint one thing that was the key to closing the deal, what was it?*

Sample Interview Questions About Real Sales Situations

> ❧ *How would you describe your sales style?*

> ❧ *What's your prospecting style? How do you get new customers?*

> ❧ *We are in a tough market. What are you going to do if customers become even more cautious about committing and sales get even harder to make?*

> ❧ *What type of customers do you find the most challenging to sell to, and how do you approach them?*

> ❧ *What would you say to our customer who quotes a lower price from our competitor?*

14 Tips for More Productive Interviews

1. Do whatever you can to relax the candidate. Welcome her warmly and offer her a beverage. Generally speaking, the more relaxed the candidate is, the more open and candid she may be, and the more valid the information you'll obtain.

2. At the beginning of the interview briefly explain the interview process. Say, for example, that you will be asking the candidate questions for about 45 minutes and then you will give her an opportunity to ask you questions about the company and the position.

3. Have at least three people individually interview the sales candidate.

4. Conduct most of the interviews in a quiet office where you won't be disturbed. But conduct at least one of the interviews out of the office, so you'll see how the candidate comports herself in different venues.

5. Interview finalist candidate on several different days and at different times to see whether she is sharp both early in the day and late in the day.

6. Talk to the candidate over the phone at least once. It will enable you to hear how she sounds and sells over the phone.

7. Give the applicant a short case study describing a sales situation and ask her what she might do as the next step in the sales process and why. This is intended to help you glean how strategic and creative she is as a salesperson.

8. Have finalist candidates accompany one of your top sales-people on one or two sales calls. Tell the candidate that this will be a great way to see what the job entails firsthand and for one of your team members to see her in action. Debrief your team member and the candidate following the sales call.

9. Always carefully check references and, using the Internet, check the candidate's background, credibility, and credit.

10. Remember that while you're interviewing the applicant, she is interviewing you and making judgments about your company. Be enthusiastic as you tell her about your company and the position before taking her questions.

11. Take notes on the candidate's responses and comments so you or the other interviewers can follow up in subsequent interviews.

12. Pay attention to the questions the candidate asks you. Are the questions thoughtful and important, or are they ones that suggest the candidate did not do any research on your company?

13. Keep an open mind and refrain from making a decision about the candidate until you have concluded the interview. This will help you listen better and provide you with more data on which to make your decision.

14. Immediately after the candidate leaves, go through your notes and write down any other impressions you have of her. Pay special attention to any unanswered questions or inconsistencies.

Recruiting and Hiring the Right Salespeople Takes Time and a Focused Approach

To hire the best salespeople, you'll need to "pick up and turn over a lot of rocks" before you'll find truly qualified candidates. Look for candidates who have demonstrated sales success in the past, and whose habits suggest they have a high work ethic—that is, they make more phone calls and set up more face-to-face calls than other salespeople—and enjoy doing so. Look, too, for candidates who have demonstrated that they have strong organizational skills, analytic skills, communication skills, problem-solving skills, and the ability to interact with a diverse group of high-powered people on both the customer side and internally. In most sales positions, particularly those that require extra effort and time to close a complex sale, salespeople will encounter numerous obstacles, so you'll want to look for candidates who maintain their enthusiasm, persistence, and focus, and enjoy developing lasting customer relationships.

Strategy 16

Realign and Reassign Territories to Boost Your Sales Team's Revenue

Approximately 20 percent of salespeople make their quota because of the richness of their territory rather than the strength of their selling skills.

— Ron Volper Group 2010 Sales Study

"I'll quit if I don't get some territory relief!"

After recovering from the sting of this threat from one of my hardest-working salespeople, I asked what he meant by "territory relief." As a rookie regional manager, I hadn't thought much about the territories in my region, as they had been in place for many years, and, as most sales managers do, I took them for granted.

The frustrated rep explained that, though he always made his quota, he felt that his current territory held far less potential than other territories. To prove his point, he showed me several charts that supported his claim that he was getting shortchanged regarding his sales territory. Finally, he promised that if I assigned him any of the other 10 territories in my region, he would increase sales and earn much more in commission. As he put it, "It's a win-win!"

Of course, I didn't want him to quit, so after presenting his case to the VP of Sales, I got the go-ahead to reconfigure his territory. Not only did he stay with our company for many years and become the top salesperson in my region, but this experience taught me an important lesson as a sales manager: Many sales territories are not the right size.

Territory Assignments Need to Be Reviewed

The Ron Volper Group Sales Study revealed that approximately 40 percent of salespeople were assigned too large a territory with too many accounts to cover. It also found that a few salespeople had territories that were too small with poor sales potential. In another study of 4,800 sales territories from 18 different companies in four industries reported on by business management experts Adris Zoltners and Sally Lorimer in the *Journal of Personal Selling and Sales Management*, 56 percent of the sales territories were either too large or too small. In their study, Zoltners and Lorimer asserted that poor alignment of sales territories cost companies 2–7 percent in sales revenues, and that many companies lose millions of dollars annually because of out-of-balance territories. They concluded that the sales lost by reducing the size of large territories was more than made up for by the incremental sales gained by increasing the size of smaller territories.

The Ron Volper Group Sales Study supports that conclusion. In addition, our analysis suggested that, after the quality of the product and the skill of the salesperson, the next-most-critical factor in determining a salesperson's success is the potential of the territory. However, even experienced sales managers underestimate its importance and often fail to balance territories.

Realigning Sales Territories

When a sales manager hires a new sales team, she has no choice but to carve out territories or at least formulate a policy as to how accounts are assigned. However, in the overwhelming majority of cases where territories already exist, many sales managers often keep them as is.

Territories need to be realigned regularly because of both internal and external factors. Internally, your company may

168

have changed its strategy or tactics, or sold off or acquired new products. Externally, one or more of your largest accounts may have relocated to a different part of the country and it no longer makes sense for the same salesperson to call on them. Similarly, if all of a salesperson's accounts are concentrated in a given industry and there is some dramatic change in that industry, such as deregulation, there may be a need to adjust the number of salespeople calling on those accounts.

Here are some indications that it may be appropriate to realign your sales territories:

» Your company is not making its annual revenue or profit goal.

» More than 30 percent of your salespeople are not making their quota.

» Different salespeople in the same territory fail to make their quotas for that territory for two or more consecutive years.

» More than 60 percent of revenue comes from existing accounts.

» Salespeople do not attempt to contact 10 percent of their accounts or do not get in to see 25 percent of their accounts.

» A large number of companies return your products, or a large number of companies that order your products don't meet your credit requirements. (This may indicate that the salesperson is pushing product on accounts that don't qualify for it, because there are not enough accounts in that territory that qualify for your company's products.)

» You add or lose several major customers or many minor customers in a territory.

» You add or lose several salespeople.

» You launch new products.

Why Are Territories Not Realigned More Often?

If there are visible signs indicating the need to realign territories, then why are some sales managers reluctant to do so? Part of the answer is that what's best for the overall company may not be in the best interest of an individual salesperson. For this reason, reassigning sales territories may create conflict between sales managers and salespeople. For sales managers, realigning territories can be time-consuming, especially if they have not done it before and are afraid of being perceived as unfair or showing favoritism.

However, in most cases, it is salespeople, not managers, who resist the change because they fear that they will make less money and have to work harder if they have to give up their existing accounts. For example, I still remember how upset I was as a salesperson when my manager told me I would lose several of my best accounts so that he could carve out a new territory.

The Benefits of Realigning Territories for the Company and Salesperson

There are many potential benefits to realigning territories for both the company and the salesperson. They include:

» Increased revenues because more salespeople cover more accounts with stronger sales potential.

» Improved competitive advantage because of a salesperson's ability to learn about new opportunities sooner.

» Improved morale of salespeople based on perception that accounts are equitably assigned and the likelihood that more salespeople will hit their quotas.

» Increased retention of salespeople because more of them make their numbers.

» Enhanced customer service and more referrals.

» Better account coverage and reduced travel costs.

» Increased number of sales calls.

» More calls spent on best accounts, and fewer calls made on low potential accounts.

» Better penetration and cross-sales of accounts.

Options for Assigning Territories

As a sales manager, you have several ways you can assign sales territories. Here are the most popular models.

Geographic

Sales managers assign accounts by zip code. This is the easiest way to split up a territory, especially in urban areas or where industries are centrally located. Depending on the size of the territory, the number of potential customers, and the nature of the product or service, more than one salesperson may cover businesses in the same zip codes.

Industry

Sales managers assign accounts based on their SIC code— that is, the industry codes used to classify business types (such as banking, insurance, high technology, or pharmaceuticals). For example, major companies such as HP and GE assign salespeople who are industry specialists to call on companies in specific industries because they know their terminology, understand their problems and opportunities, and are more credible in recommending their company's products.

Key Accounts

Sales managers assign a salesperson a few large accounts with substantial potential. For example, some salespeople may be given only one account, such as ExxonMobil, Wal-Mart, or the federal government, because their potential is so large. Moreover, because the revenue potential is usually greater for a larger account, companies may be more willing to spend a greater share of their budget to have salespeople travel to them.

171

Medium and Small Accounts

Medium and small accounts often have different challenges and opportunities than larger ones and they need to be approached differently, which is why some companies have a separate sales group call on them. In this case, small and medium-sized customers feel special when salespeople and their companies offer them the same respect and customer service they show to their larger accounts.

Named Accounts

Rather than assign salespeople a piece of real estate, some sales managers provide their salespeople with a specified list of current accounts and potential new accounts to call on during a given year.

Unassigned Accounts

Salespeople can call on any account within a geographic area. In this model, the first person to meet with that account (and document it in a call report or add that account to a pipeline forecast) gets to have it. For example, in a retail environment, such as for an auto dealership or for a company that sells time shares, salespeople take turns selling to new customers who walk through the door, although existing customer relationships are usually honored. Customers in these environments will sometimes hear salespeople ask, "Who's up next?" which means which salesperson will handle the next customer.

Additional Options Regarding Sales Assignments

As the head of sales or sales manager, you'll also want to decide whether or not to:

» Divide your salespeople between sales executives who prospect for new customers and account managers who manage relationships with existing customers.

» Create an inside sales team to sell to smaller accounts over the phone or Internet, as opposed to face-to-face selling.

» Pair off salespeople to include an inside telephone rep and outside rep.

Are Your Salespeople Generalists or Specialists?

The issue of whether to have a *generalist sales organization,* in which all salespeople sell all products, or a *specialist sales organization,* in which one group of salespeople sell one product or product line, and another group another product line, has been debated for decades. The answer depends upon the specifics of the situation.

The advantages of a generalist sales organization are:

» Reduced cost of travel.

» Saved time for the sales organization.

» Saved time for customers.

The advantages of a specialist sales organization are:

» Better knowledge of the product(s) and their application for a customer.

» Salesperson perceived by customers as more of a consultant who can provide more added value.

» Increased penetration of accounts by having two salespeople from the same company learn about and meet customer needs.

One of the key determinants in deciding between the generalist and the specialist sales approach is if the customer in a given company is the buyer of both product lines. If so, then the likelihood is that the customer would rather not have to spend time meeting separately with two different sales reps from the same company. On the other hand, if there are two or more different buyers for the two or more product lines within that company, then this is not an issue. In a tough economy, however, in order to reduce the cost of travel and thus the total cost of sales, more companies have opted for a generalist sales approach.

How to Implement the Realignment

Although some salespeople will inevitably be uncomfortable losing accounts, you can make the task less contentious by doing the following:

» Give salespeople several months' notice that you are going to realign territories.

» Involve salespeople to the extent practical in the realignment.

» Give salespeople who lose accounts revenue credit for any accounts they called on and forecasted in their pipeline that closes for approximately three months after they lose the account.

» Have the salesperson who will give up the account introduce the new salesperson to the account (and make note of how professionally he did this in his performance review).

Building the Territory Around the Strength of the Salesperson

Rather than first creating the territories and then assigning salespeople, another option is to custom-build the territory around the strengths of the salesperson. Here are some factors to consider in this regard:

» Where does the salesperson live in relationship to her territory, and how much time and cost can you allow the salesperson to incur in traveling to customers?

» What are the salesperson's preferences as to the type of accounts she will call on?

» What is the salesperson's experience in and knowledge of specific industries, and with which industries and accounts is she likely to be most credible?

» Does the salesperson have prior contacts within certain accounts?

» With which level and department will the salesperson be interacting, and with which customers will the salesperson be most credible?

A Fresh Face in a New Territory Can Dramatically Increase Sales

In some cases, it may be beneficial to reassign a few accounts rather than reassign whole territories. For example, if a salesperson has been unable to get an appointment with an account for an entire year, consider having her swap that account with another salesperson in exchange for a different account, especially if the travel costs are similar. Sometimes this is done to encourage all salespeople to make contact with all of their accounts, but in many instances it's done because some salespeople are better at interacting with some types of customers than others. Occasionally, you may need to reassign an account because the salesperson and the customer clash. Even if it's not the fault of the salesperson, it's usually best to assign a fresh face to the account. A more radical alternative is to have salespeople swap whole territories. Sometimes shaking up things results in increased revenues for both salespeople. In most cases, savvy sales managers use a combination of methods for reassigning territories so that everyone has the best opportunity to increase their sales and commissions.

Strategy 17

Protect Your Sales Team's Golden Selling Hours

In a survey of a randomly selected group of 850 salespeople in 12 different industries, we found that reps with average sales spend approximately 35 percent of their available time selling, whereas salespeople who are top performers spend a minimum of 50 percent of their available time selling.

— Ron Volper Group 2010 Sales Study

"Everybody, stop what you're doing. I need you to get to work on *this* right now. It's a top priority!"

These were the all-too-common words our sales team heard from one of the more frustrating sales managers I worked for early in my career. The results of his frequent and ill-timed interruptions during our most productive selling time were: (1) more mistakes and incomplete orders, (2) a decline in team morale (based on the silent collective groan whenever he stepped into the sales office), and most importantly (3) a decrease in sales.

Given the limited time salespeople have to make calls, sales managers need to make sure that they do not do anything that takes away from their most precious resource—their "Golden Selling Hours." Otherwise, frequent interruptions, untimely meetings, or poorly planned last-minute tasks will make selling in a down market even more difficult and reluctant customers less likely to buy.

176

Golden Selling Hours Are Less Than You Think

It's a useful exercise to calculate with your team how much time in one year each salesperson actually has available for selling:

Days in a year		365
Weekend days	102	
Holidays	10	
Vacation days	15	
Sick or personal days	5	
Days of conferences or meetings	13	
Days of training	5	
Less total		(150)
SELLING DAYS		215

But wait. That's not the end of the story, because even more time to sell slips away. A small number of customers will meet with salespeople at 7 a.m. or 7 p.m., but most customers will only schedule appointments between the hours of 9 a.m. and 3 p.m. And although some enjoy having lunch with salespeople, most reserve the lunch hour for themselves. So even assuming that salespeople can meet with customers—who are cautious about spending their time (and money) in a down market—any time during this six-hour period, even this time is eroded by other factors outside the salesperson's control. These factors include:

Daily travel time between appointments	60 minutes
Waiting time for customer appointments	30 minutes
Salesperson's lunch time, including travel to and from lunch	60 minutes
TOTAL LOST TIME	150 minutes

177

This means that two and a half hours need to be subtracted from the approximate six hours customers are available in a typical day (from 9 a.m. to 3 p.m.). This lost time does not include the inevitable emergencies and other obligations, such as doctor's appointments, meetings with kids' teachers, and traffic delays, during the prime selling hours that further reduce available time. Thus, because of their own schedules, family obligations, customers' schedules, and other unavoidable "time-wasters," salespeople typically wind up with only three and a half hours per day in the 215 days available for selling.

12 Things Sales Managers Can Do to Maximize Their Reps' Golden Selling Hours

1. Only hold sales meetings when you have important issues to discuss, and schedule them at times that are least intrusive to your reps' Golden Selling Hours.

2. Coach your reps to use times other than their Golden Selling Hours to complete sales reports, check on orders, handle customer problems, answer questions, mentor newcomers, and follow up on or initiate internal requests.

3. Jointly review individual reps' proposals, presentations, sales reports, and forecasts before or after their Golden Selling Hours.

4. Periodically review reps' itineraries to help them eliminate wasted travel time.

5. Ask your reps to confirm appointments with customers.

6. Although they can be great for building rapport, limit long lunch or breakfast meetings with reps.

7. Strategize with your reps their next step in the sales cycle so they can better define sales call objectives and compress the sales cycle.

8. Stick to your allotted time for both team meetings and individual meetings with your reps.

9. Schedule brief weekly meetings on a set day and time with each salesperson on your team to assess his or her time-management effectiveness and suggest ways to overcome time-wasters.

10. Provide your reps with pre-approved boilerplate sales reports, proposals, and other frequently used documents so they can concentrate on making sales.

11. Write clear and concise e-mails with a request for a return receipt to communicate detailed procedures, schedule changes, and technical or product information to your team.

12. Have your sales team use contact-management software and other sales-related programs and provide them with appropriate training.

Sales Managers Can Avoid These Common Time Traps

Like all sales managers, as a VP of sales I faced, many situations that gobbled up my time. However, I was able to decrease wasted time by using what I call the *–ation* categories. Here are a few common time traps and ways you can deal with them:

Time Trap: *"I can't find it. Give me another copy."*

Nothing is more frustrating and wastes more time than when a boss, rep, customer, or sales manager says, "I can't find the report (memo, product info, and so forth) you gave me yesterday. Can I get another copy, or can you resend it to me?"

Organization: Keep tracking sheets of who you gave what to and when. In addition, have backup files with extra copies of electronic and hard-copy documents, so if anyone needs an additional copy of something, you can easily find it.

Time Trap: *"I'll do it myself."*

Delegation: Micro-managers may think that they can do it better themselves. Even if that's true, the reality is that there are not enough hours in a day for even the most efficient sales manager to do it all. The solution is to delegate tasks with a clear set of guidelines and expectations to sales assistants, customer service reps, and others who can competently complete them to your satisfaction. Also, for projects comprising an extended time period, check in with reps periodically to answer any questions, and be sure they are on track.

Time Trap: *"This is the third time I've had to explain this!"*

Information: If you find yourself repeating instructions to your reps then try this alternate approach. Get the necessary information and clear instructions to complete a given task to the reps before explaining it to them. For example, if your company is launching a new product or going through a procedural change, e-mail the details in a memo a day or two before hosting a meeting to discuss the new product or protocol.

Time Trap: *"I'm spinning my wheels."*

Motivation: The Ron Volper Group Sales Study of 2010 revealed that many sales managers who work extremely long hours without a break do not necessarily increase their company's sales. In fact, in many cases they were less productive, made more mistakes, had more staff problems, and had an increase in sick days and turnover. If you're working on a lengthy project or proposal and running out of steam, reward yourself by calling a friend or going out for a quick cup of coffee when you complete it, or even when you complete a difficult part of it.

Time Trap: *"My to-do list is a mile long."*

> **Combination:** Too much to do and too little time to do it is a common complaint of many sales managers. So, where you can, combine related activities and eliminate irrelevant or redundant activities. For example, answer some e-mails while you and your rep are waiting to see a customer.

Let Your Reps Sell When They Have the Best Chance for Success

Make it your goal to use your time more efficiently and coach your reps to use their time more productively. Find a balance between assigning your sales team necessary tasks and allowing them to figure out the best time to meet with or be in touch with their customers. As the economic health of their markets change, so may the buying patterns of their customers. For those reps whose customers are reluctant to buy because their industries are in down markets, it is more important than ever for reps to maximize their Golden Selling Hours. Let them sell when they have the best chances of reaching their customers and closing deals, and you'll have happy reps, happy customers, and a happy boss.

Maximize Your Sales Team's Intellectual Capital

The companies that survive and thrive when markets are down are the ones that encourage their sales teams to gather, analyze, and use intellectual capital to determine how they need to adapt to change.

—Ron Volper Group 2010 Sales Study

Founded in 1859, by 1930, the Great Atlantic and Pacific Tea Company (also known as A&P) had grown to 16,000 grocery stores and more than $1 billion in sales, making it the third-largest company in America. For the next 80 years, it sold products that everyone needed. However, in 2010, it filed for Chapter 11 bankruptcy. What happened?

Although many factors caused its demise, a major reason was its failure to learn about and act on several trends that began long before its recent bankruptcy. In the 1940s, most A&P stores were located in cities, but after World War II, many Americans purchased cars and moved to the suburbs. They used their cars to go food shopping, but because there were few A&P stores in the suburbs, consumers started shopping in other newly opened supermarkets, such as King Kullen. At the same time, many consumers purchased refrigerators, freezers, and other kitchen appliances that enabled them to buy, prepare, and store more and larger food items, so they did not need to shop as often. Even so, A&P's smaller stores carried fewer items and smaller-sized items than their competitors, and, as a result, their market share declined. In addition, television replaced radio as a way to entice millions of consumers to try new food brands they saw advertised on their favorite programs and endorsed by celebrities. These brands became popular, but A&P stores did not carry them, instead sticking with the A&P house brands. Not surprisingly, many consumers preferred the more widely advertised brands, with predictable results. Although there were other factors at play, many experts believe that A&P's bankruptcy can be attributed to its failure to learn about and adapt to changes in consumer buying habits and emerging trends.

A&P was not alone in its failure to learn about and adapt to changing consumer habits and tastes. Only 14 percent of the companies that were listed on the Fortune 500 in 1959 were still on the list 50 years later, in 2009. Many of them went out of business; others saw their revenues shrink so much that they were de-listed and replaced by larger companies. The moral of the story? Learn about and adapt to your customers' changing tastes and buying habits, or go out of business.

Savvy Sales Managers and Companies Promote the Gathering of Intellectual Capital

Savvy companies, such as Apple, Google, Amazon, and IBM, achieved their spectacular success because they promote learning and adaptation to change. Not only do Apple products enable Apple customers to capture and store information, but the company itself collects and analyzes data to learn about its customers and market segments, and create products that meet changing customer needs and wants when markets are up and down. Apple learned from their sales reps that they could create a huge market of loyal customers at a time when nervous customers were notoriously fickle and reluctant to buy by supplying quality technical help for their products. I'm one of those customers.

Not long ago, I spilled soup on my iPad, so I frantically called the salesperson that had assisted me with my purchase. He told me to come into the store and one of their "Apple geniuses" in the tech department would see to it right away. When I joked to the receptionist at the store, "I need to talk with your genius with the highest IQ," she directed me to the "Genius Bar" where one of Apple's "geniuses" cleaned up my iPad—good as new. I was a happy and relieved customer. Apple's added value service reinforced my decision to buy their product.

When Sales Are Down, Use Your Sales Team to Increase Your Intellectual Capital

Even seasoned salespeople can lose their motivation in a down market if their sales decline. To mitigate this problem, put your sales team to work gathering information about:

- » Changes in their respective territories and local markets.
- » Changes in existing customers' needs and wants.
- » Changes in new customers' buying behavior.
- » Emerging industry trends.
- » Complaints and challenges related to new technology.
- » Complaints and kudos for competitors' new products and services.

At a time when customers are ever more cautious, and have more product and service choices, increasingly what sets salespeople and their companies apart is their intellectual capital—that is, how effectively they collect and analyze information about their tactics and strategies, learn from their successes and failures, and adapt to the changes in their markets, customers, and competitors to continuously improve their products, their processes, and their people. The most profitable companies are now the ones that are not content with an "if it ain't broke, don't fix it" strategy, but instead continually look for new ways to improve what they do—and better serve their customers. By encouraging their salespeople to learn as much as they can, these companies provide their customers with even more added value.

Create a Learning Center for Gathering Intellectual Capital

Many larger companies that recognize the value of knowledge as a strategic asset for salespeople and others often have their own learning centers. For example, GE has one in upstate New York; Xerox in Leesburg, Virginia; and Qwest Communications, near Denver. These and other well-regarded companies have state-of-the-art learning equipment, comfortable dormitories, and cafeterias at their learning centers. But you don't need to be a sales manager in a Fortune 500 company to promote learning; even small companies can set aside rooms for training and education in their corporate offices and elsewhere.

Resources and Strategies for Salespeople to Gather Intellectual Capital

Top salespeople and their companies use the following resources and strategies, among others, to gather intellectual capital and gain insights into the economy, their markets, and their customers' preferences:

» Territory and account reviews.

» Call reports and call summaries.

» Monthly forecasts and reports.

» Planning retreats.

» Monthly business reviews.

» Weekly sales huddles and monthly sales meetings.

» Annual or semi-annual company-wide meetings.

» In-house seminars for salespeople and others.

» Customers' evaluations of their salespeople.

» Analysis of competitive wins and losses and lessons drawn from them.

» A director of sales training that reports to the head of sales.

» Periodic meetings with other affiliates or subsidiaries in their company to trade information about new trends, risks, opportunities, and so forth, and see how various business entities within the same corporation may be able to collaborate to sell more of their products and services.

The Big Picture of Intellectual Capital: Factors That Affect Markets and Sales

Many trends have changed which products and services customers buy, how they buy them, and the way companies now need to sell to them. The expansion of technology, with the advent of the Internet and social media, including LinkedIn, Facebook, Twitter, and others, has produced a profound change in how companies communicate with their customers and market their products. Some of the newer trends that sales teams and their companies may want to think about as they consider their product and service offerings, their approach to their markets, their organizational structure, their strategies and goals, and their budgets, are:

Consumer Demographics

❯ Decline in the birthrate, especially among middle- and upper-middle-class families in the United States and other industrialized countries.

❯ Baby Boomers hitting retirement age.

❯ Increased longevity and aging of the population in the United States and elsewhere.

❯ Increased diversity in the United States and an increase in the percent of minorities, especially Latinos living and working in the United States.

> Increase in the percent of females in college and in many professions, such as law and medicine.

Consumer Economics

> Global recession and uneven economic recovery.

> Major increase in the price of oil and other commodities such as gold.

> Major decline in most of the residential and commercial real estate markets in the United States.

> The decline in manufacturing in the United States.

> The economic ascendancy of China and its status as a creditor nation and the second-largest world economy.

> Increased trade with emerging markets in Brazil and India.

> The massive debt of certain countries in the European Economic Community, such as Greece, Portugal, and Ireland.

> Growing concern about the United States debt.

Consumer Values

> Increased awareness of and attention to people's impact on the environment, and the need to recycle and use scarce natural resources judiciously.

> Increased concern with health, physical fitness, and lifestyle.

> Increased concern about global security and threats from disaffected people and groups.

> Less trust of political and corporate leaders.

Consumer Financial Situations

> Major increases in the cost of health insurance and medical care.

> Increased credit card debt among American consumers.

> Weaker financial condition of many states.

- Substantial increases in cost of college tuition.

- Increased number of people renting instead of owning their homes.

- Consumer savings has increased but is still lower in the United States than in many other industrialized countries.

- More major U.S.–based companies, especially consumer goods companies, earning an increasing percent of their revenues from overseas markets.

Employment

- Major increase in unemployment and underemployment in the United States and elsewhere.

- Increase in number of freelance and contract workers.

- Increase in number of people who telecommute.

- Increase in self-employment and number of small businesses.

- Decline in union membership and the power of unions.

- Less loyalty from corporations to employees and vice versa.

- College graduates having more difficulty finding jobs.

Consumer Buying Habits

- Rapid growth in online sales and consumer comparison shopping.

- Better informed customers.

- Less customer loyalty to companies and salespeople.

- Less customer loyalty to brands and increased buying of generic products.

- Consumers having more choice and more leverage in a sales interaction.

- Decrease in number of consumers using intermediaries, such as travel agents, real estate agents, and financial consultants, to purchase products.

> Greater difficulty of salespeople getting through to intended contacts on the phone because of voice response systems and voice mail, and getting through via e-mail because of spam filters and so forth.

Promoting a Learning Sales Organization in a Down Market

To maintain and build a learning sales organization, as a manager or executive you need to encourage salespeople to contribute to your company's intellectual capital through formal reports, brainstorming sessions, and presentations, but also through informal talks over breakfast, lunch, or a cup of coffee. Once salespeople offer their ideas, you and other team members must provide them with feedback; otherwise they will feel that they've wasted their time. Follow up solid ideas with "pilot tests" and then evaluate the results. That way your company will be able to assess new ideas and approaches before implementing them, and the salespeople who developed the ideas will get the credit they deserve.

18 Ways to Facilitate Your Sales Team's Learning

1. Create "swat teams" that specialize in generating ideas to improve your products, sales, and service.

2. Establish a "sales boot camp 101" for new hires and advanced sales boot camps for experienced team members.

3. Create a "buddy sales" system so that buddies can help one another stay on track for their numbers and brainstorm ways to overcome objections.

4. Use social media such as Facebook and LinkedIn to build relationships with a diverse group of customers and to test new sales ideas.

5. Send selected salespeople to outside seminars and have them report what they learned to the rest of the team.

6. Reimburse salespeople, sales managers, and others for attending MBA programs.

7. Sponsor sales managers and others to attend executive education programs at universities.

8. Obtain subscriptions to business and industry newspapers, magazines, journals, and so forth (such as the Wall Street Journal, Financial Times, The Economist, Fortune, Forbes, and Inc.).

9. Have your sales team discuss customer comments on surveys.

10. Conduct employee attitude surveys.

11. Benchmark your sales team against those of other companies to see how effective and efficient they are, and how they can improve their performance.

12. Rather than simply completing and sending sales reports to management, have sales team members analyze their activities and results.

13. Attend and present at industry conferences, and report back to your sales team.

14. Participate in various industry, business, professional, alumni, and community groups.

15. Join a Mastermind group.

16. Attend a business book discussion group.

17. Be a mentor or mentee for another manager.

18. Shop customers and competitors and report back to your sales team.

Intellectual Capital Is the Key to Increasing Sales in a Down Market

Albert Einstein defined *insanity* as "doing the same thing over and over again and expecting different results." Savvy sales managers know that if they want to increase sales in a down market, their sales team will need to gather and assess what the data and experiences tell them. Learning leaders encourage salespeople to gather and assess what the data and their experiences tell them.

But that's not enough. They need to do things differently based on what they learn. As a result, these salespeople perform their jobs better than their competitors, are more productive, and are better prepared to be promoted into the next job. These team members become your top sales performers because they are up for new challenges even when their markets are down.

Increase Your Sales With Motivating Compensation Plans

In almost every case, the salespeople who left their companies joined other companies that paid them more.

—Ron Volper Group 2010 Sales Study

It *is* about the money!

Several years ago, my firm was retained by a well-regarded hospitality industry association to conduct a study of why high-performing salespeople—the people companies want to keep—left their company. The association's hypothesis was that high-performing salespeople leave not because of compensation, but because of other factors, such as lack of professional growth or dissatisfaction with management. In our study, entitled *Turning Turnover Around,* we found the opposite.

Though there were a range of factors that affected "unforced turnover" the number-one reason—by far—was unhappiness with their compensation. And in almost every case, the salespeople that left joined companies that paid them more. In subsequent years, we did an analysis of turnover in other industries and came to the same conclusion. Armed with this knowledge, managers need to look at their compensation plan.

15 Signs That Your Company Needs to Redesign Its Compensation Plan

There are several indicators that suggest your compensation plan is not serving your company or your sales team well and should be re-designed.

1. Your company is not reaching its revenue or profit objectives.

2. You company's revenues or profits have not increased over the previous year.

3. More than 30 percent of salespeople have fallen short of their revenue goal.

4. Your cost of sales is more than 20 percent of net sales revenues.

5. There are not enough prospects in the sales pipeline and not enough new business.

6. Your sales team has not met its goal for multi-year contracts.

7. Your company's annual turnover of salespeople is more than 20 percent when markets are up and down.

8. Your best salespeople have left the company.

9. A compensation survey indicates that your company pays significantly less or more than your competitors.

10. Your salespeople cannot readily explain the compensation plan.

11. Your salespeople express dissatisfaction with the plan throughout the year.

12. Your salespeople are not calling on the right target markets.

13. Several top salespeople turned down your offers for a sales position with your company.

14. Salespeople can't reconcile their incentive compensation payment with what they believe they sold for the period covered.

15. Your company has different compensation plans for different salespeople.

Create a Compensation Plan That Aligns With Your Marketing Goals

Successful sales managers know that the best compensation plans are those that align the salesperson's activities and rewards with the company's annual and longer-term goals and strategies. That means, for example, if the company's primary goal is to take market share from competitors, then salespeople should be paid most aggressively for bringing in new accounts from the competition. If, on the other hand, the company's priority is profitability, then salespeople should be paid most aggressively for the margins on their sales. If a sale of a new product represents the most critical win for the company, then salespeople should receive additional compensation for selling that product.

Pros and Cons of 3 Different Sales Compensation Plans

There are dozens of variations in sales compensation plans, but they usually fall into one of three categories: straight salary, commission only, and a combination plan. Let's look at the advantages and disadvantages of each sales compensation plan.

Plan 1: Straight Salary

Salespeople receive a fixed rate of monetary compensation regardless of the number of sales or amount of revenue generated. None of the compensation is at risk as long as the salesperson is employed.

Advantages	Disadvantages
Supports salespeople when their market is down.	Difficult to recruit and retain sales stars.
Company can accurately forecast annual costs.	Salespeople may not make as many calls, or work as hard as necessary.
Encourages salespeople to go the extra mile in after-sale support.	Rewards the least-productive salespeople.
Simple to administer.	May yield less upside revenues.
Avoids revenue disputes.	
Supports salespeople doing reports and other non-selling activities.	
Facilitates teamwork.	
Provides salespeople with a predictable income.	

Plan 2: Commission Only

Salespeople's compensation is based entirely on sales revenues (and/or the company's margin on sales).

Advantages	Disadvantages
Maximizes revenue production and sales activity.	Less after-sale support and weaker customer service from salespeople.
Pay is fully aligned with most of the company's goals, and is linked to performance.	Salespeople may be too pushy with customers.
Attracts the most aggressive salespeople.	Higher turnover and lower salesperson loyalty when markets are down.
May yield upside revenues (as salespeople work harder to close sales).	Less cooperation in doing reports and non-sales activities.

Plan 3: Combination or Mixed Plan

Salespeople receive a fixed salary plus the opportunity to earn variable compensation (commissions and/or bonuses) based on their sales results.

Advantages	Disadvantages
Easier than a straight commission plan to attract salespeople.	More difficult to administer than straight salary.
May encourage high levels of productivity.	Increases company's fixed costs for payroll.
Protects salespeople when their market is down.	May give salespeople mixed messages.
Salespeople are more willing to complete reports and administrative duties than with a straight commission plan.	

Most Successful Companies Use the Combination Plan

Although the straight salary and the commission only plan offer certain advantages, companies that are the most sales-driven and have grown their revenues and market share the most usually use a combination plan (also known as a "mixed plan"). As a result, they tend to be the most successful at attracting and keeping the top-producing salespeople. However, the more challenging issue for sales managers is how to structure the combination plan so that it works best for your company and salespeople in a down market.

Part of the answer to this question depends on what your competitors are paying, and how they structure their compensation plan. For this reason, it's valuable to engage a firm to conduct a salary survey for your industry. Keep in mind, however, that in trying to land sales talent, you're sometimes not only competing with companies in your industry, but also with companies in other industries.

A second factor regarding compensation is to identify what the job of salesperson entails at your company, and how much they directly control sales. For example, in some cases, the salesperson's role is to serve as an account manager, where he is mainly responsible for managing existing relationships (being a "farmer"), as opposed to bringing in new business (being a "hunter"). In other cases, even where the salesperson does bring in new business, his success may be attributable to the fact that his company has the best brands, or the best products, or the best advertising and marketing support, and the salesperson is essentially showing up and taking orders.

A third factor regarding compensation, and especially the incentive portion, centers on the amount of revenue and the profitability of the business that the salesperson brings in. For example, a salesperson selling jet engines, with a long sales cycle, should be compensated more generously than one selling pharmaceuticals or janitorial products.

How Much Variable vs. Fixed Compensation?

As a rule of thumb, I suggest that you structure your combination plan so that salespeople receive at least 40 percent of their total compensation when they hit their goal in variable compensation—that is, commissions and bonuses, as opposed to their fixed compensation, or base salary.

17 Elements to Consider in Designing Your Compensation Plan

1. Assign All Salespeople Revenue Goals.

Your compensation plan is most aligned with your company's plan and therefore most effective if you assign all salespeople revenue goals (quotas). The goals should be for annual production, but also include monthly quotas. If your business is at all seasonal, assign different revenue goals for different months, based on the prior years' results. Make the quotas challenging, but also make sure they are realistic and attainable, or you will run the risk of "de-motivating" your sales team. In developing quotas, seek the input of salespeople, but let it be known that you make the final decision based on many factors, including the company's budget and need for growth, the prior year's revenue and profit for a given territory, its revenue potential, and the tenure of the salesperson.

2. Eliminate Caps on Compensation.

Though some companies may have trouble doing so, most companies would do themselves a favor by eliminating caps on compensation. If you cap your compensation, you are inadvertently telling salespeople that they should stop selling when they reach a certain level of revenue.

3. Freeze Base Salaries.

Because you want salespeople to earn the lion's share of compensation based on results, not for showing up to work, I recommend that you freeze base salaries.

4. Adjust Salespeople's Base Salaries to the Published Cost of Living in a Given City.

Because it's more expensive to live and work in some areas of the country than others, level the playing field and create equity for a national sales team by adjusting salespeople's base salaries to the published cost of living in a given city.

5. Have All Salespeople Work Under the Same Compensation Plan.

Special compensation plans for particular salespeople will create confusion and resentment. Plus, federal and state laws mandate "equal pay for equal work," so make sure that all salespeople work under the same plan.

6. Guarantee Part of Their Incentive Compensation.

In recruiting salespeople, and especially sales stars, it's appropriate to guarantee part of their incentive compensation, but do not let the guarantee exceed six months.

7. Base at Least 90 Percent of Incentive Compensation on Objective Criteria.

At least 90 percent and ideally 100 percent of the incentive part of a compensation plan should be tied to objective, measurable results. No more than 10 percent of their compensation should be based on subjective criteria, such as teamwork, completion of reports in a timely manner, and other administrative tasks. Otherwise, you'll be accused of having favorites and weaken morale on the sales team.

8. Pay Quarterly Bonuses for Meeting Quarterly Quotas.

To heighten motivation and encourage salespeople to bring business forward, pay them a bonus for meeting quarterly quotas, in addition to monthly commissions.

9. Pay Salespeople a Commission on an Escalating Basis for Each Dollar They Bring In.

Here is an example of an escalating commission based on a range from 1 percent to 11 percent on the annual level of sales:

» 1 percent on the first $200,000 in revenue.

» 2 percent on the next 200,000.

» 3 percent on the next 200,000.

» 4 percent on the next $200,000.

» 5 percent on the next $200,000.

» 7 percent on the next $400,000.

» 9 percent on the next $400,000.

» 11 percent on all revenue after that.

If you're locked into paying high base salaries, you can mitigate this by establishing a revenue threshold that salespeople need to reach to qualify for commission payments. Let's say for many years you've been paying your salespeople an annual base salary of $100,000 and all your competitors are paying a base salary of $75,000. In most instances, you would not suddenly cut your base salary by $25,000. However, you could establish a threshold, based on the amount of revenue a salesperson would have to bring in to earn the initial $25,000 in commissions.

10. Pay a Higher Incentive for New Business Than for Repeat Business.

If feasible, pay salespeople a higher incentive for new business versus repeat business (as it usually requires more time and a higher level of skill).

11. Don't Quibble About Where the Sale Came From.

Don't try to divine whether the deal just came in over the transom, or whether the salesperson actually produced it. If it's from an account in his territory, pay him.

12. Pay Compensation in a Timely Fashion.

Pay salespeople for their achievement as soon after they bring in the business as possible. That means paying them the following month for the previous month's production. Similarly, pay them their bonus check for meeting their quarterly revenue goals in the month immediately after the quarter ends.

13. Pay Salespeople for Results, Not Activities.

Though you want to coach salespeople to make as many (quality) sales calls as they can, only compensate them when they make the sale. Similarly, as the manager, you'll want to encourage teamwork, but you should not pay for it. The fairest plan is one that pays each salesperson for what she produced, not on how well she "works with others." You'll obtain that through strong leadership and coaching, not by "bribing" salespeople to do what they should be doing anyway.

14. Keep the Compensation Plan Simple.

Include between three and five elements, so salespeople can maintain focus.

15. Have Salespeople Read and Sign the Compensation Plan.

Have each salesperson read and sign the compensation plan to acknowledge they have read it and will be paid based upon it. Doing so will reduce disputes.

16. Develop a Governance Document for the Plan and Share It With Each Salesperson.

The governance document describes the plan, defines terms (such as "new" and "repeat" customer), and discusses the policies and procedures regarding:

» Eligibility (who is eligible and when).

» Formulas for compensation and split commissions.

» How disputes will be settled and who makes the final decision.

» What happens with the commission when a salesperson leaves the company.

» Whether and under what circumstances the compensation plan can be discontinued or changed.

» Whether salespeople will be paid when the business is booked, the product is shipped, the service performed, or the invoice is paid.

» How it affects salespeople's commissions if the customer fails to pay for the product or service.

The issues of when salespeople qualify for incentives and what happens if they leave the company can be especially contentious. A few state courts, for example, have apparently ruled that if a company ships the product, or books the sale as revenue, the company cannot withhold commission from salespeople. Regardless of how courts rule on these issues, it would seem to be in everyone's best interest that you clearly delineate your company's policies.

17. Retain the Company's Option to Change or Eliminate the Compensation Plan.

Although you hope never to have to do so, include a statement in your plan saying that the company can change or eliminate the plan at any time at its sole discretion.

6 Steps to Designing a Successful Compensation Plan

Now that you know what to keep in mind in designing your plan, let's look at the six-step process you can use to develop a successful plan.

Step 1: Establish a Compensation Task Force

A compensation task force might consist of the vice president of sales, the chief financial officer, selected sales managers, several top-performing salespeople, the director of human resources, and the director of information technology. You may want to consider retaining an outside consultant to help you design it or provide a broader perspective on what other companies are paying and on the best compensation plan for your company.

Step 2: Review the Current Compensation Plan

Because certain aspects of your current compensation plan may be working, confirm why you are changing the current plan and how the company will measure the success of the new plan. Get agreement on the company's annual and longer-term goals and check to see how well the current compensation plan is aligned with them. Identify the elements that suggest that any shortfalls in sales may be related to the current compensation plan, as opposed to product issues, marketing issues, or hiring issues.

Step 3: Design the New Compensation Plan

Align the new compensation plan with your company's strategic objectives and marketing goals. Take special care to incorporate the "17 Elements to Consider in Designing Your

Compensation Plan" (described on pages 197-202) when creating your compensation plan. Model the new compensation plan against the current plan to test compensation levels under both plans. Look carefully for any unintended consequences of changing the plan. Once you have a draft of the new compensation plan, circulate it to a select group of colleagues who represent the people affected by the plan to ensure there are no ambiguities or unintentional outcomes, and to measure its potential level of receptivity among your sales team. Be open to suggestions and be willing to make any needed revisions.

Step 4: Communicate the Plan

Craft compelling materials to market the compensation plan to the sales team, including the purpose of the new compensation plan and how it compares with the compensation plan it replaces. Introduce the new compensation plan the way you would launch a new product so that it gets the sales team's enthusiastic support.

Step 5: Assess Impact

Once your company implements the compensation plan, have the compensation plan design team analyze the results under the new compensation plan and compare how people would have been paid under both plans. Compare the compensation plan's actual costs to budgeted costs. Compare results to the previous period and note any sales increases or benefits along with sales decreases or drawbacks. Other ways to assess the impact of a new compensation plan is to compare turnover rates, and survey salespeople and sales managers for their reaction to the new plan versus the old plan. Determine if customer compliments or complaints have increased or decreased under the new compensation plan.

Step 6: Celebrate Success

Recognize top performers formally and informally. Acknowledge their contributions before their peers. Present them with both checks and symbolic rewards such as with plaques, trophies, pins, or rings at a recognition dinner or similar event.

The Final Test

Finally, here are four simple tests to determine the success of your sales compensation plan in a down market:

1. You only have to explain the plan once and everyone on the sales team understands it.

2. The majority of salespeople say the plan is fair.

3. Sales revenues increase from the previous year.

4. Your top-performing salespeople turn down job offers from other companies.

When It Comes to Compensation Plans, It's All About Performance

A well-designed compensation plan is like a high performance automobile: It's a powerful vehicle that management can use to drive sales and arrive at its financial destination. A winning compensation plan attracts and retains top-performing salespeople—the essential element of every growing company. So take the time to figure out the best compensation plan for your sales team and design one that is truly road-warrior worthy.

Strategy 20

Recognize and Reward All Your Salespeople

Most salespeople are motivated by two things:
pay in the pocket and pats on the back.
—Ron Volper Group 2010 Sales Study

It was some 30 years ago, but I remember it like yesterday. In spite of a down market, my company rewarded me along with several other sales-contest winners, by inviting us to join the president and senior vice president of sales for dinner at Sam Lord's Castle—on the Caribbean island of Barbados! At the dinner our senior vice president got up in front of us and our spouses to talk about what each one of us had done to increase sales in a tough economy and qualify for the trip. What made the event so special was that after our sumptuous dinner, the winners of this sales contest got to spend several more days enjoying this tropical paradise.

Not only do I remember that incentive trip, but I remember the sale I made that put me over the top and qualified me for the trip. Even today, when I think about that sales contest, it brings a smile to my face. Although recognition and rewards programs—including sales contests—need not be as expensive or as elaborate as the one in Barbados, many companies fail to use them. As a result, they miss an easy opportunity to enhance their salespeople's morale and boost their sales.

Use Contests to Boost Sales and Motivation

Recognition and rewards programs consist of all the things your company does each year to motivate and focus salespeople, including your sales compensation program, sales contests, and how you praise and celebrate the achievements of your salespeople. Whereas your sales compensation program is intended to remain in place for at least one year, and sometimes many years (and constitutes a more formal agreement between your company and your salespeople), sales contests work best for shorter periods of time and are less formal. Recognition in the form of praise can take place in formal situations, such as annual conferences and award dinners, as well as in informal situations, such as monthly sales meetings, in company newsletters, or even in a personal conversation.

Your sales compensation plan is intended to support your company's longer-term marketing vision and goals, whereas sales contests can be used to make mid-course corrections in sales behavior. Think of it this way: Compensation plans are the main rockets that launch your spacecraft into orbit; sales contests are the smaller rockets that can be used in route to get you back on course if your team deviates from their planned route. Here are some common situations that benefit from a well-designed sales contest:

» Your sales team is too reliant on repeat business and needs to develop more new business.

» Your sales team needs to boost sales of a specific product without diminishing sales of their other products.

» Your sales team is not getting a sufficient number of multi-year contracts that yield long-term revenues.

What Motivates Your Salespeople?

Most salespeople are motivated by two things: pay in the pocket and pats on the back. Of course, a solid compensation plan is an absolute must, but money is only part of what it takes

206

to keep salespeople happy and productive. If you want all of your sales team—not just the top performers—to go the extra mile and make that one extra call, you'll want to fuel their motivation by developing an annual recognition and rewards program. In a down market, when competition is tougher and sales often are smaller and take longer to close, it's even more important to do what you can to keep their spirits and their activity levels up.

In working with thousands of salespeople, I've learned that most top salespeople work for both intrinsic and extrinsic rewards. The intrinsic reward is the satisfaction they derive from building a relationship with customers, helping them solve a problem or taking advantage of an opportunity, and closing a sale. That is, they are driven to succeed because of their own professional pride. Their feelings of confidence and self-worth (what the American psychologist Abraham Maslow called *self-actualization*) are intensified if their achievement is also acknowledged by their manager. If you celebrate their achievement in front of their peers, they'll feel even better about it and themselves.

How a Recognition and Rewards Program Can Help Your Company

A recognition and rewards program need not be expensive, and it can help your company to:

» Increase the sales team's productivity and results.

» Attract and retain top salespeople.

» Increase salespeople's motivation, so they'll try even harder.

» Focus salespeople on the most important activities and results.

» Reinforce or complement the incentive compensation program.

» Inject fun into their work environment.

Even if your company has a recognition and rewards plan, it may need to be revised if:

> » There is little or no increase in sales, sales activity, or team morale.

> » Salespeople do not pay attention to the plan.

> » Disputes arise about the mechanics of the plan.

> » High turnover of salespeople, especially among top performers.

> » Rewards and recognition to salespeople are late.

> » You incur high cost with little revenue gain.

Conversely, the marks of an effective recognition and rewards plan are:

> » It's easy to implement and manage.

> » Salespeople like it and enthusiastically support it.

> » It increases the desired sales activity or the intended result.

7 Ways to Develop or Revise a Recognition and Rewards Program

Whereas an incentive compensation plan's goal can be to increase overall annual sales, that is too broad a goal for a sales contest. However, the process for designing a sales contest as part of recognition and rewards program has some similarities with the one you use to develop an incentive compensation program.

1. Appoint a Task Force

The task force typically consists of the head of sales, some sales managers, the heads of HR and IT, and some high-performing salespeople. The task force should address the:

> » Purpose of the contest.

> » Ground rules of the contest.

> » Time frames of the contest.

» Mechanics of the contest.

» Rewards of the contest.

» Recognition of the contest.

2. Determine What Behavior or Result You Want to Achieve

During normal economic times, I would wait until the end of the first quarter to introduce a sales contest. However, while managing a talented sales team during a time when the market was down, I knew I needed to get them out of the gate quickly. To that end, I implemented a "Fast Start Sales Contest" to give salespeople who landed business in January an extra *spiff,* or an immediate bonus for a sale. As a result, we had our best January in the company's history without a falloff in sales during February and March.

3. Design the Plan and the Contest

The best-designed sales contests are short and simple, and last anywhere from a few weeks to three months. Complicated or lengthy contests that try to reward too many things weaken their impact. Pick one important goal that you think your team can achieve within a time frame of no more than three months and reward only one or two behaviors or results. To avoid ambiguity and disputes, make the goal measureable and objective. For example, you can reward the most face-to-face sales calls or the most sales for a certain product, but you should not reward the "best sales call," because that's a matter of opinion.

Also consider whether you want individual salespeople to compete against each other or pit one sales team against another. In many instances, if the incentive plan rewards individual achievement, it can be useful to have a contest that rewards teams. Regarding sales contest themes, many companies build their contest around a season, such as Halloween, or a sports theme, such as baseball or basketball (think of March Madness), the Indianapolis 500, or the Kentucky Derby. A little imagination can go a long way to make your sales contests fun and effective.

209

4. Model the Financial Impact

After designing the plan, model its financial impact under various scenarios, so you will not be caught off-guard or over-budget. Remember that sales contests are used to augment your company's sales compensation plan—not replace it—so you do not need to allocate a lot of money for them.

5. Introduce the Sales Contest With the Appropriate Fanfare

Because a sales contest is not intended to have the same importance as your incentive plan, you can announce it with a light touch, but, at the same time, you should talk it up and make sure everyone knows about it. The goal of the implementation is to get the salespeople's attention and support, and have them see it as a fun way to earn a pat on the back or a modest reward.

6. Track, Manage, and Support the Contest

Many companies make the mistake of implementing a sales contest, but then do nothing to support it. If you as the manager forget about it, so will your salespeople. After you introduce it, you need to track the results either weekly or monthly (depending upon the length of the contest and what you are tracking) and circulate the results to the sales team. In some of the best-run contests, the manager communicates the interim results via a special newsletter.

7. Celebrate the Contest Winner's Success

Make a big deal about winning the contest and recognize the winner(s) with a great deal of enthusiasm. Play up the contest, and announce the winner in your company's newsletter or, if possible, create a special contest newsletter. Can you imagine how the contest winners would feel if they also received a letter or a phone call from your CEO or other senior executive congratulating them? Another option is to have the CEO invite the winner(s) out for dinner. Wow—talk about impact! One approach to recognition that worked for me was to appoint sales contest winners to my Sales Advisory Committee. They felt honored to serve on it, and I felt fortunate to have them as a sounding board.

Tangible Rewards Are Cash, Merchandise, Perks, and Time Off

Will you award business perks, such as a choice of parking space, or choice of shifts in a call center, or first dibs on vacation schedules? If you're interested in having tangible rewards, you can offer cash or cash equivalents (such as gift certificates), merchandise, tickets to a sporting event or entertainment, magazine subscriptions, or even a trip (if the contest is for a big prize).

For salespeople who sell lower-ticket items, you can offer free movie passes or small gifts. If merchandise, you can select the item or provide the salesperson with the opportunity to select it from a catalog. Some incentive companies will manage the entire merchandise program for you. It's not hard to do it internally. You can offer business-related merchandise, such as an iPad, briefcase, or leather binder, or something more personal, such as an iPod or sound system. Years ago, I was thrilled to win an entire Sony Stereo system. And, at a time when very few people had them, I was once awarded what was then called a "car phone." You can even provide a special service, such as having a limousine pick up the winning salesperson at home and drive him to his appointments for a specified period of time.

Another reward that some salespeople appreciate is paid time off. This reward may be more attractive to salaried salespeople than those on full commission or combination plans, because many commissioned salespeople would rather not miss an opportunity to add to their sales revenues. You can also incorporate an element of chance into the sales contest. For example, salespeople who meet certain revenue targets get to draw prizes from a fishbowl. A good way to get buy-in from your salespeople is to involve them in the selection of rewards (keeping in mind that you'll want to give them budgetary guidelines).

Symbolic Rewards Bestow Honor, Status, and Praise

If the award is symbolic, you can give the winning salespeople plaques, trophies, certificates, or other symbols of success. I once was awarded a metal sculpture that vaguely resembled Rodin's sculpture of *The Thinker* (if he had sculpted it blindfolded!). As ugly as it was, I proudly displayed it on my credenza for many years. Ford and AT&T have rewarded star employees by featuring them in their television commercials. Qwest Communications honored its top call center salespeople by placing their pictures in a sales training program that we developed.

Informal Recognition Publicly and Privately

Besides sales contests, many leading companies do a great job of informally recognizing their salespeople and those people who support them. In my long career in sales management and consulting, I have never found an instance where a salesperson felt she received too much praise. As long as the praise is warranted, salespeople appreciate it. As a manager your job is to catch your salespeople doing something right—and to thank them for it. Look for opportunities to praise them before their peers.

3 Easy-to-Implement Sales Contests That Build Morale, Teamwork, and Sales

Here are three fun and effective sales contests that you can use right away to increase your sales and team morale.

1. Fast Start

The purpose of this contest is to encourage salespeople—some of whom may be recovering from the year-end festivities—to get off to a running start and make as many sales calls and bring in as much business as they can early in the year.

How it Works: First post pictures of winners of the Kentucky Derby, the Indianapolis 500, and Olympic track stars under a banner that says "Fast Start." Then call a brief meeting and announce that the salesperson who signs the most contracts in the first month of the year will win the Fast Start contest, and have his or her normal commission doubled for the month.

When I ran this contest, it really worked! Several salespeople had their best January, and as a team we had a record January and an excellent first quarter. We celebrated by going to a game arcade where we had fun driving race cars at the "Grand Prix."

2. Steak and Beans

The purpose of this contest is to spur sales of a new product or a product that is not selling well.

How it Works: During the introduction and training on the new product, announce that the salesperson who most exceeds revenue goals for sales of that product within a given time, while meeting all his or her other revenue goals, will win two tickets and transportation to a local professional team's game. Be sure to get the tickets before you announce the contest.

When I ran this contest, I chose our local pro football team. I attached $11'' \times 17''$ color copies of the two tickets on the office wall to remind my salespeople about the contest. When the contest ended, I called everyone into the conference room, where I arranged for two cheerleaders from a local school to dance in and announce the winner with great fanfare. The contest (and cheerleaders) were a big hit—and our product launch was a success!

3. Recruiting Rock Stars

The purpose of this contest is to have your team members recommend outstanding salespeople to fill several new sales territories.

How it Works: At your national sales meeting, bring in a local rock band to play while you are socializing or having dinner. Announce that your department is looking to hire additional salespeople who are "rock stars" and that team members who recommend salespeople that you hire will win two tickets to attend any concert of their choice.

When I ran this contest, several of my team attended the same concert as the winner, so it turned into an even bigger and more motivating contest.

Recognize and Reward Everyone on Your Sales Team

Successful sales managers know that building their company's revenues is a team effort. Therefore, remember to appropriately recognize and reward not only your top performers, but also those salespeople who are struggling either because the overall market is down or because they are having trouble penetrating their specific market. Regardless of the reason for a sales slump, it's important to encourage and look for ways to praise those salespeople if you want to keep their confidence up even though their sales or commissions may be down. For example, if they are adding qualified accounts to their pipeline, even if they are behind in their numbers, it's important to pat them on the back. As the leader of your team, if you are generous and genuine with your recognition and rewards program, your sales team will appreciate their recognition and work even harder for their rewards.

Conclusion

◇

Cautious customers change their buying behavior when good economies shift downward. Now you know how to respond because you have learned 20 of the most powerful strategies I know for salespeople to sell more in down markets and for sales managers to build productive sales teams that bring in more revenue.

When you offer your products and services with the confidence that you can address every question and overcome every objection of cautious customers who are reluctant to commit to a sale, then you will achieve my goal in writing this book: to help you *Up Your Sales in a Down Market*.

Index

About the Author

R ON VOLPER, PhD, is the founder and managing partner of Ron Volper Group, Inc., a 25-year-old management consulting firm based in White Plains, New York, that specializes in sales effectiveness. As a consultant and speaker for more than 30 years, he has helped more than 90 Fortune 500 companies and other medium-sized businesses in the United States and abroad increase their sales. As a nationally recognized authority on business development, he has helped field sales teams and call center salespeople develop and expand relationships and accelerate their profitability in both good and tough times.

Ron has served as the top-producing salesperson, a regional manager, and as vice president of sales and marketing for two Fortune 500 Companies. He has been a frequent keynote speaker and has addressed more than 200 businesses and industry associations.

Ron has been interviewed on Bloomberg Television, CNBC, and MSNBC on several occasions, and he has been quoted in *Fortune Magazine*, *Inc.*, *Bottom Line Business, Nation's Business, Success, Accounting Today*, and *Manufacturing News*.

Ron holds a bachelor's degree in English and Economics from Queens College, and earned his master's degree from Indiana University, and his PhD in media and communications from New York University. He is also an adjunct faculty member at New York University, a Certified Toastmaster, and a winner of several speaking contests. Ron is active in numerous other organizations, including the National Speakers Association, where he was president of the New York Chapter and recipient of the Presidential Leadership Award.